ADVANCE PRAISE

"Buy it; read it; call in the Alchemist."
Guy Nixon, Founder & CEO, GoNative.com

"A brilliant bible for business."
Ruth Kennedy, Director, Kennedy Dundas Limited

"Andrew Wallas throws out the rule book,
go with it, you will not regret it."
Gavin Hughes, Executive Chairman, Project Fortis

"A game changer and must-read for any leader. Business
Alchemy provides the magic dust in my toolbox."
Carole Gaskell, Founder & CEO, Full Potential Group

"A refreshing and inspiring read; it challenges us to take
brave steps to allow the magic – or alchemy – to happen."
Robin Bayley, Author and Storytelling Consultant

"A pioneering approach to radical change in business."
Jo Bamford, Director, JCB

Published by
LID Publishing Ltd.
Unit 204, The Record Hall, 16-16A Baldwins Gardens,
London, EC1N 7RJ

31 West 34th Street, 8th Floor, Suite 8004,
New York, NY 10001, US

info@lidpublishing.com
www.lidpublishing.com

A member of:

BPR
Business Publishers Roundtable

www.businesspublishersroundtable.com

Printed in the Czech Republic by Finidr
ISBN: 978-1-911498-24-7

Cover and page design: Caroline Li

ANDREW WALLAS

BUSINESS ALCHEMY

EXPLORING THE INNER, UNSEEN DYNAMICS OF THE BUSINESS

LONDON   MONTERREY
MADRID   SHANGHAI
MEXICO CITY   BOGOTA
NEW YORK   BUENOS AIRES
BARCELONA   SAN FRANCISCO

FOR BRIAN STANLEY

CONTENTS

ACKNOWLEDGEMENTS

My first business mentor was Brian Marsh OBE. He taught me a great deal. My first guide on my inner journey was Dr John Denford. He opened many doors which I had previously determined to keep closed forever. Since that time, I have benefitted from many teachers and guides, some of whom I would like to formally acknowledge now:

Ruth Kennedy, Audrey Pasternak, Carole Gaskell, Lara Fares, Victoria Fuller, Fiona Arrigo, Emma Cannon, Gavin Hughes, Guy Nixon, Steven Rimmer, Caroline Philpott, Melanie Renwick, Dave Lee, Mark Miller, Tony Barker, Lizzi Luminati, Matt Murton, Monika Barton, Jane Priceman, Charisse Basquin and Helene Hook, all of whom have shown me tremendous support.

Charles Pasternak, Michael Wood, Jim Jackson, Gerard Hughes S J, Steven D'Souza, Brigitte Sumner-Djie, Ray Butler, Marie Butler, Arjuna Ardagh, Chuck Spezzano, Shomit Mitter, Ralf Marzen, Sander Kirsch, Jacques Berliner, Guy Gladstone, Albert LaChance, Samadarshiniji, Anandagiriji, Ross Hyslop, Hugo Arranberg Yuri Zhivago and Humphrey Arranberg Pasternak, all of whom have taught me much about life and business.

Rob Cottingham for trusting me unreservedly.

I would like to thank and acknowledge my editor at LID, Sara Taheri for greatly improving the manuscript, and Martin Liu, general manager at LID, for providing me with this opportunity to express my views to a wider audience.

But most of all, I would like to acknowledge, honour and thank my wife, Anna Pasternak, for her enduring support, patience, tenacity, inspiration and love. Without her, there is no doubt, that not one word of this book would ever have been written.

Over the past few months, whilst finishing this book, I completed a significant financial transaction in the financial services sector within the City of London, with Brian Marsh, with whom I first worked 45 years ago. So the final words belong to T S Eliot:

"What we call the beginning is often the end
And to make an end is to make a beginning.
The end is where we start from.

....

We shall not cease from exploration
And the end of all our exploring
Will be to arrive where we started
And know the place for the first time."

Little Gidding
The Four Quartets

INTRODUCTION

Most business books, executive coaching and leadership development are approached from the perspective of teaching a theory or formula that improves performance. If you are looking for a business manual or detailed theory on how to implement change in your business, then do not buy this book.

Business Alchemy is not formulaic and does not follow a predetermined path; it is experiential. It has to be experienced to be fully understood. It is concerned with identifying the hidden aspects of your business that block performance, as well as its infinite possibility and potential. It is not rooted in facts and knowledge, but in intuition and magical possibility. This book puts forward a different approach to business that is reflective and resonates with a different level of inner knowing.

Throughout the book, we will be engaged in a creative tension between rational thought and heartfelt wisdom or gut instinct. Individuals and organizations tend to polarize at one end of the spectrum or the other. Very few are prepared to entertain a dance between these radically opposing forces, thereby missing the opportunity to create alchemy.

CHAPTER ONE

BUSINESS
AS
ORGANISM

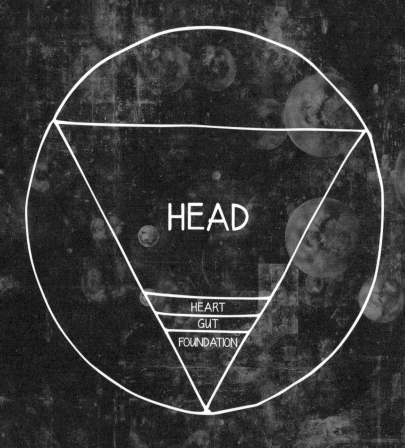

HEAD

HEART
GUT
FOUNDATION

CORPORATE CULTURE

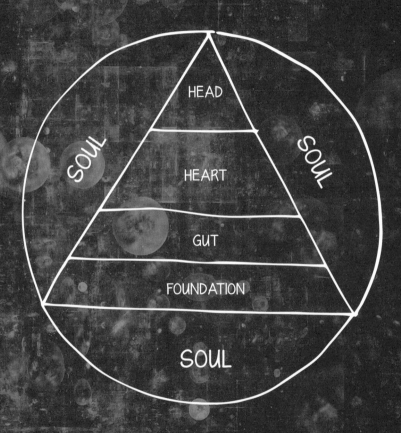

BUSINESS ALCHEMY

We are driven by analytical, logical thinking and a rational approach in most aspects of daily life, particularly within most structures and organizations. Every business is a living organism with an identity. Larger companies spend millions of pounds seeking expert advice to help them create and reinforce their corporate identity. Part of the perceived wisdom within the corporate world is that a strong brand identity is essential for a successful business. One of the realities of corporate life, certainly in the Western world and probably the world over, is that it is very mind-dominated. Of course, it is also true that the wider culture we have created is also mind-dominated. The identity of the business is closely aligned with the mind of the business. There is less and less room for the heart or heartfelt decisions, for trusting gut instincts, and for the soul and soulful reflection.

There is, of course, nothing wrong with rational thinking, logical analysis and factual argument. There is great value in this approach. However, we have become totally out of balance and out of sync with the natural rhythms of life and a huge amount of our potential. As individuals, organizations and cultures, we are operating a long way short of our capabilities and hence, we are not reaching fulfilment.

As individual men and women, we need to learn to listen more to our hearts. Most people I meet are very disconnected from their hearts. It takes practice and commitment to learn to live more from the heart. Imagine a heart-led organization: what would this look like? A rational, logical, mind-dominated business is focused on doing, is didactic, driven and competitive. There is no question that all organizations need these qualities. A heart-led business creates space to pause and listen. It is not didactic and competitive, but rather reflective and collaborative. It is interested in listening to the rhythm and mood of the situation and then acting decisively. A heart-led organization values intuition, contrary views and instincts that might not initially make sense.

When I go into a business, I often create a space and stillness within me so that I can listen to the heartbeat of that business. Depending upon the contractual engagement with the client, at an early stage in my work I will often gather senior executives and ask the question repeatedly, "What is the heartbeat of this business?" or alternatively, "What is the heart of this business?"

It is fascinating to me that the executives who are gathered have rarely asked this question before, nor reflected upon it. This process of enquiry always reveals an insightful, varied discussion, which energizes and animates those present. There is a lively debate with many contrary views, but it is interesting that there is usually a moment in time when views converge, and there is a landing and agreement between colleagues as to the real heartbeat of the business. For example, when working with a large, successful public relations company, after half a day of exploring answers to these questions, the executives understood that the heartbeat of their business was creating connection. In the same way, when working with a corporate law firm, a similar process revealed that the heartbeat of the business was protecting and defending the rights of others.

I often read about and observe large organizations that go through a substantial downturn. It is well documented that Tesco, having had an uninterrupted period of growth over ten years, then suffered a serious contraction in revenue and profit. I remember thinking at the time that this was an example of a business that had become preoccupied with, and driven by, quarterly returns and voracious shareholders. I have not worked with this company, but it seems to me that the heartbeat of Tesco should resonate with supplying quality food to ordinary households. Many will argue that the situation with this company is more complicated and multi-layered, but I maintain that by disconnecting from the heartbeat of a business, the rot begins to set in. The great paradox of this situation, which is a well-trodden pathway in large businesses, is that of course every business wants to increase revenue and profit. However, becoming fixated upon this achieves the very thing you are trying to avoid. If, instead, the business listened to the heartbeat and was influenced by this inner pulse, then the revenue and the profits grow as a consequence and by-product of being attuned to the heart of the organization.

As individuals and as organizations, we need to learn to value the heart and to rebalance the mind-heart relationship within our businesses. This can only be done by learning to listen to our hearts. With a rational approach, a mind-dominated enterprise, it is possible to create handbooks, procedures and formulae that, once understood by others, allow them to execute and implement these principles within the organization. It is different with the heart. You cannot create a handbook or formula for listening to the wisdom of the heart.

After 40 years of working with individual entrepreneurs, groups and organizations, I have witnessed time and again moments of alchemical shift that are non-logical and do not make sense, but create a profound change in both the organization and the individuals concerned. In Sanskrit[1], one of the oldest languages on the planet, the two principles behind the universe are *Ra* and *Ma*. Ra is masculine and Ma is feminine. Ra is where we get the word 'rational'. And Ma is where we get the word 'magic'. As businesses, we have become overly rational, and we need more Ma; we need to get a bit of the magic back. This is about rebalancing. It is not about devaluing or getting rid of rational thinking and ending up with some New Age fantasy business driven by unrealistic and shallow affirmations. It is about valuing the role of the mind – rational, logical and analytical thinking – as well as respecting the way of the heart and embracing intuition, creativity and wisdom.

Even in the most rational, logical, analytical community that exits – the scientific community – many major breakthroughs occur after years of research hit a brick wall or dead end and cease to provide a desired outcome. The brilliant minds at work sit back and give up, exhausted, and in opening up that space there is a moment of insight, an epiphany similar to the most famous example: the 'Archimedes' moment[2].

Certain cultures, organizations and communities hold gut instinct in high regard more than others. History is littered with examples of military leaders, politicians, scientists, inventors and businessmen and women, who, when faced with stressful and conflicting situations, have trusted their gut instinct much to their own and others' benefit. Caesar's decision to take his army across the Rubicon and into Rome in 49 BC was based upon a gut feeling rather than political or military analysis[3]. Churchill regularly operated on gut instinct, especially at the end of May 1940 when two of the most senior members of his War Cabinet – Lord Halifax and Neville Chamberlain – urged him to make peace with Hitler[4]. His gut instinct told him not to and he listened.

Gorbachev is another example of a politician who relied upon gut instinct. In 1986, he introduced *perestroika* (restructuring) and *glasnost* (freedom of speech) into the USSR[5], and followed this up two years later by allowing Eastern Europe to regain its independence. These three examples show that men of courage who relied on their gut feelings were able to change history: Caesar's defiance of the Senate led, after his death, to the founding of the Roman Empire. Churchill's determination not to sue for peace resulted in Britain and its allies, not Germany, winning World War II. Gorbachev's reforms initiated the dismantling of the Soviet Union. Most politicians, in contrast, are 'calculators'.

Modern travel and expeditions (the South Pole, Mount Everest and the moon) are all carefully planned. In contrast, Morton Stanley's gut feeling in 1876 that the Lualaba River in Central Africa was the source of the Congo (whereas David Livingstone had speculated that it might be the source of the Nile) was proved to be correct when he navigated all the way to the Atlantic, not the Mediterranean. Columbus' gut feeling (based on vague speculation) that the earth was round resulted in him sailing westward for China, and he was eventually proved correct. Acting on gut instinct whether in art, travel, war, politics or business, has been eroded since the turn of the 19th century – in favour of deliberation. However, every successful businessperson with whom I have met has always had highly honed intuition and gut instinct, upon which they have relied time and time again, even if they would not call it this (which many do not).

Overly rational and logical businesses tend not to trust gut instinct. They would, of course, argue that this is with good reason! Gut instinct can be wrong or appear to be wrong. Around the boardroom table many difficult, seemingly complex dilemmas are fiercely argued with contrary points of view. Often an individual board member has a strong gut instinct on the best way forward, but suppresses this due to fear of ridicule. If an organization can encourage voicing the instinct of the gut, then not only will it enrich the debate, but it will invariably lead to a better outcome. Within a Western culture, we have not been conditioned to trust our instincts. Over many decades, through education and family systems, we have learned to devalue this vital ability. While gut instinct regularly saves lives, people still find it difficult to trust it and fear being let down by it. The truth is that for every business the best rational, logical and analytical research will also invariably let them down from time to time.

The irony is that as the human race has evolved through agricultural and industrialization and created so-called civilized communities, we have exalted rationality as a way of consciously and unconsciously separating ourselves from other species. This has been done in the pursuit of reinforcing a sense of superiority, both intellectually and culturally. We forget that we are part of the animal kingdom and that we have been given instincts for good reason. All species rely upon instinct for survival and many so-called primitive communities thrive and prosper with a better balance between rationality and gut instinct. Thankfully, over the last 50 years, our post-industrial Western cultures are beginning to look back to indigenous cultures and reclaim this ancient wisdom.

In my experience in working with companies, the most difficult area for a business to make authentic progress in is learning to trust the gut instinct during critical debate. However, when I have worked with companies over a longer time, they have demonstrated an ability and willingness to relearn this vital capacity. Allowing and encouraging senior executives to voice gut instinct and have colleagues create the space to reflect upon this invariably proves beneficial to decision-making and hence performance.

As a living, breathing organism, every business has a mind, a heart, a gut and a soul. One of the basic divisions within companies are those businesses that fall into the category of 'do not mention the soul' and those that welcome the idea of the soul with scepticism or curiosity. My conviction and my experience have taught me that every business has a soul. However, I am not in any way attached to the word 'soul'. In many cases, when working with a business, I substitute the word 'essence' for the word 'soul'. I am always curious and interested in discovering the essence of a particular business. For example, if we take an individual and we give their 20 closest friends an unlimited supply of paper and ask them to write down all the characteristics of their friend, the aggregate of these attributes would not fully encompass the essence of that person. We somehow know the essence without being able to fully articulate it. The same is true of a business and of a country and anything else in life. For example, take Greece. We could invite 20 or 30 regular visitors to this country to write down all the characteristics and attributes of this beautiful ancient Mediterranean land. The results would not fully capture the essence or soul of Greece.

The essence or soul of a business is linked to the idea, first introduced by Aristotle, that the whole is greater than the sum of the parts[6]. We all intuitively know this to be true. More than 30 years ago, when I was studying philosophy and learning about the pre-Socratic philosophers, my tutor gave me an enduring example of this. Suppose you call a garage and order a brand new Mercedes Benz S Class[7]. You wait more than two months for delivery and get home from work one day to find approximately 30,000 car parts scattered all over your lawn. You are confused and then angry. You call the Mercedes dealership and ask what the hell is going on. The pedantic dealer persistently asks, "What is missing?" A rational man would eventually have to admit that there is in fact nothing missing. Every part of a Mercedes Benz S Class has been delivered to the agreed-upon address. It is the way in which these parts are arranged in conjunction with each other that creates the car. This is a wonderful example of the truth that the whole is indeed greater than the sum of its parts.

Frequently, when working with a business, a radical starting point is to gather the executive team and ask, "What is the soul of this business?" or alternatively, "What is the essence of this business?" Just as in the case of enquiring about the heart or the heartbeat of the business, this invariably leads to an animated discussion. It is a different enquiry to an exploration of the heartbeat of a business. It is diving deep into the essential nature of the business. Sometimes this resonates with the question: "What is the raison d'être of this business? Why did this business come into existence and why does this business continue to exist?" Again, many varied and contrary views and opinions are expressed. Having been through this experience with numerous companies, I am still surprised and delighted when that moment arrives and there is a shared collective knowing in the room that we have articulated, as closely as possible, the essence or soul of this living organism that forms such a major part in the lives of the executives present.

This shared knowing presents a real 'ah-ha' moment, which is jointly experienced between the most senior executives of the organization. Why is this so important? Once we discover the soul of the business, this becomes the compass and litmus test in every meeting, including board meetings and strategy debate when there are critical decisions to be made. It is a priceless tool in the managing and development of any successful business.

At the heart of *Business Alchemy* is the mission to bring the mind, the heart, the gut and the soul of the business back into balance and alignment. *Business Alchemy* is not negative about the mind or rational thinking. It is critical of organizations and businesses that are out of balance and limiting their potential. *Business Alchemy* transforms an organization by reconnecting it to its heart, gut and soul.

HOW TO REBALANCE YOUR BUSINESS:

1. Take time to explore the heart of your business.

2. Listen to the gut instinct in your business.

3. Create space to discover the soul of your business.

4. Rebalance your business by bringing the head into the right proportion with the heart, gut and soul.

_____

_____

_____

_____

_____

_____

_____

_____

_____

_____

_____

_____

_____

_____

CHAPTER TWO

SIMPLICITY

At the heart of Business Alchemy is the principle of simplicity. The longer I have been working with businesses and the older I get, the more convinced I am that every aspect of life is incredibly simple. Each and every business, irrespective of size, is essentially simple. For example, banks take deposits and lend money, supermarkets sell food, while retailers are in the business of distribution. Equally, human beings, the main driver in a business, are also simple. However, as we know, human beings complicate all aspects of life. One of the overriding consequences (and possibly a key motivation) of complication is staying stuck. It is like living within a maze; we appear to find a new way forward or a new way out, only to discover that we are back where we started. If we are truly honest with ourselves, much of our lives, including our business lives, fall into this category. We spend huge amounts of time and energy rearranging the furniture of our lives without ever really achieving fundamental change. Why is this?

First, businesses are created and managed by human beings. Each one of us has a tripartite brain, which has evolved over millions of years. The largest and oldest part of the human brain is the reptilian brain, which is 300 million years old. For the first 100 million years of our evolution, reptiles ate their offspring and did not create a relationship with any other member of their species or any other species. The second part is the mammalian brain, which was created 100 million years later and is now 200 million years old. It was not until the mammalian brain was formed that relationship existed. With the introduction of mothers suckling their young, a relationship was created for the first time. The third part of the human brain is the neocortex or frontal lobe system, which is approximately 20,000 years old. The frontal lobe is the part of the brain that controls important cognitive skills, such as emotional expression, problem solving, memory, language and judgment. It is, in essence, the 'control panel' of our personality and our ability to communicate.

Each area of our brain, and our brain as a whole, operates as a 'pattern recognition programme'. This means that whenever we enter a new situation, two critical questions arise: "Have I seen this before?" and nanoseconds later, "Is it a threat or is it safe?" This is why people tend to sit in the same seat repeatedly, take the same route to work, order the same food on a menu and are generally drawn to what is familiar. Years ago, I used to commute by train to work daily and on one occasion witnessed a physical fight between two men because someone was sitting in another passenger's regular seat. Businesses, just like individuals, lean towards the familiar and maintaining the status quo. This cannot be overstated, because there is both a conscious and unconscious drive to maintain familiarity that is perceived to be safe because it is 'known'.

Second, we need to understand the nature of the mind and its comparison to the heart. The mind needs problems to solve. It has been developed and evolved for this purpose. If it does not have problems, then it feels unimportant. Individuals, as well as businesses, seek and need recognition. Over the past hundreds of years, cultures have evolved that are dominated by the mind. We have become addicted to heroic acts, to overcoming major obstacles and receiving praise for this. This is because it is our mind that gives us a sense of identity. It is a constant compulsion of the ego to create difficulties that need to be solved. It is exactly the same within any business or organization: there is a constant need to reinforce the sense of identity through crisis management and winning major new business accounts. It is important to understand that this is the nature of the mind. Any crisis is a huge opportunity for the ego.

Over the last 100,000 years, the development of our brain and our mind has separated us from the heart of the matter. The heart does not need a reward and seeks a pathway without drama. The only thing that is important to the heart is a successful outcome, not who gets credit for the success. This is because the heart is not interested in identity, like the ego. Being in our heart represents the absence of ego, and all business conflict is more often than not ego-driven. One of the principles of simplicity is that we need to move away from a mind-dominated culture to a heart-centred life and a heart-centred business.

At the core of the scientific community is the principle of simplicity,[8] referred to as Occam's Razor, attributed to an English Franciscan monk, William of Occam (c.1287-1347).[9] This principle, frequently invoked by scientists, states that among competing hypotheses, the one with the fewest assumptions should be selected. Occam's Razor represents the preference for simplicity in the scientific method. Alongside this tenet sits Quine's conception of Ontological Parsimony[10]. According to the principle of Ontological Parsimony, a theory that entails the existence of fewer entities or kinds of entity is better than one that entails the existence of more entities or kinds of entity, all other things being equal. This principle enjoys widespread acceptance in scientific and ordinary empirical reasoning.

Sir Isaac Newton's third law of physics states that: "For every action there is an equal and opposite reaction."[11] This echoes another natural law, the law of cause and effect. Within the Eastern tradition, we have the Law of Karma.[12] *Karma* is a Sanskrit word that means action, work or deed. This refers to the universal principle of cause and effect underlying the cosmos. As Albert Einstein said, "If you can't explain it simply, you don't understand it well enough." We are all familiar with both businessmen and women, and academic men and women, who get off on jargon and complication as a way of convincing themselves that they really are as clever and gifted as they believe.

Businesses spend the majority of their lives dealing with effects. Employees are busy reacting to micro and major changes that are affecting the business. Some of these effects are perceived to be totally out of the control of the business; for example, a fluctuation in exchange rate, or a geopolitical crisis involving invasion and war. Others might be recognized as being more in their control; for example, the loss of a major client, moving premises or a merger with another company. Irrespective of the perceived element of control, the business is busy dealing with the effect rather than the cause. Business Alchemy is concerned with establishing the root of the problem, not dealing with symptoms.

In my professional and social life, I am regularly interacting with men and women who are having affairs with married people. This is going on all around us and is a perfect illustration of how we create complication to maintain the status quo. If we take the example of a woman having an affair with a married man, the details will vary, but the central issues are wrapped up in a complicated story of the man's wife being fragile and having some sort of depression, the children being at a vulnerable age, that he really wants to spend the rest of his life with her, but external factors make this impossible. The timing just isn't right. Each time I am exposed to this story or a variation thereof, my response is always the same: I say to the woman that if she were to write down all the characteristics of this man that she loves and all the reasons that she continues to see him, in spite of the pain this causes, the most important reason would not be on the list. The main reason that any woman in this situation is with a married man is that she is attracted to and drawn to unavailability. Once we identify that this is the overriding consideration within this dynamic, the complexity falls away and we can treat the root of the problem, not the symptoms. In every case, if a single man were to show up and fall madly in love with her and declare that she was the woman he had been looking for all his life, and he wanted to spend the rest of his life with her, she would be beset by panic and run away. Obviously, this is equally true for men having relationships with married women.

In a similar way, the perfect illustration of a simple issue in a business environment that is made complicated is one in which a business has a major company or group of companies that are their largest client, producing a substantial percentage of their revenue. The organization is imbued with fear over the possible loss of this client. Senior executives are preoccupied with the consequences of such a loss; it would erode a substantial amount of the profit and result in expensive redundancies, as well as loss of credibility to the image (identity) of the company. The clients are well aware of the power imbalance and daily use it to their advantage.

Whenever I hear a story like this, I simply explain to the business executives that they are colluding with a bully and acting like a slave or hostage. However much they protest with expressions such as, "You don't understand …" or, "Actually, it's more complicated than that … ," I reaffirm the simple reality that the business is disempowering itself. As Eleanor Roosevelt reminded us, "No one can disempower you without your permission." The business is, of course, helping to maintain the status quo. This unhealthy dynamic permeates and affects every aspect of the business. Once we have identified the essence of this dynamic, then the solution is both simple and readily available. The executives need to value the business enough to explain to the largest client that this dynamic is unhealthy for both parties and that, unless it is changed, they would rather lose the account. This takes courage and conviction in one's own value. Individuals and businesses often do not want to see the simplicity of the scenario or indeed follow its diktats because they live in fear of the consequences. However, addressing the root cause of the situation always leads to freedom and liberation, and the creation of something new. The alternative to addressing this simple situation is to continue in an unhealthy, demoralizing, exhausting environment that can only lead to a slow death.

It's important to recognize that the businesspeople with whom I am working already know the simplicity of the situation and the healthy course of action, but cannot bring themselves to execute it because there is too much fear; the perceived risk is too great. The discomfort of the familiar is preferred over the uncertainty of the unknown. As individuals in our daily lives, as well as in small and large businesses, there are many scenarios when we are repeatedly reaffirming the perceived complication as a way of maintaining the status quo. It is like existing in a fog, but it is familiar. Therefore, to our mind and our identity, which operate as a pattern-recognition program, it is safe. There is no perceived threat because we know how to manage this situation, however uncomfortable it might get. The potential loss of the largest client or any perceived change is imbued with the energy of threat and is to be avoided at all cost. It is only by dismantling the perceived complication and exposing the simplicity that a new pathway opens up, leading to a healthier, more liberated and profitable future.

HOW TO HARNESS THE POWER OF SIMPLICITY:

1. Observe how often colleagues use the terms 'complex' or 'complicated' in business discussions.

2. Refuse to accept any situation as complicated or complex.

3. Articulate the simplicity – i.e., the truth of the matter.

4. Choose the new pathway that opens up.

CHAPTER THREE

FLOW

Every business and organization is like a river. When a river is flowing, it is full of vitality, vibrant and healthy. In this buoyant natural state, a river creates an ecosystem in which everything is interdependent. Interdependence is an important and desirable state of being. Most individuals and most businesses spend their lives oscillating between a state of dependency and independence, neither of which is effective. If a river gets blocked for any reason, then it stagnates and becomes smelly quickly. Many businesses operate within a dynamic of dependency. They are in a dependent relationship with clients and other stakeholders, and they foster dependent relationships within the organization. Middle management is overly fearful of making decisions and owning responsibility, as they are too dependent on the level of management above them. Dependency is based on neediness and creates anxiety.

At the other end of the spectrum, many businesses operate from a dynamic of independence. They are distant and aloof from clients and other stakeholders and foster a culture in which individuals and teams operate as silos and do not communicate with each other. The battle-cry of independence is: "I don't need you. I can do it better myself."

The dynamic of interdependence is the nature of partnership; i.e., we are in this together. Clients rely upon their service provider and the service provider relies upon the client. It is a mutually beneficial relationship. A chief executive relies upon a board of directors and a board of directors relies upon a chief executive. Management relies upon employees and employees rely upon management. The sales department relies on marketing, marketing on sales. The front office relies upon the back office, and the back office relies upon the front office, and so it goes on throughout the organization.

With both dependence and independence, there is a serious restriction to the natural flow. Individuals and departments become stuck in an unhealthy relationship with each other. For example, in most organizations the front office is superior and becomes independent, and the back office is seen as inferior and becomes dependent. This is an unhealthy dynamic – it keeps both parties stuck. Where there is a genuine appreciation of mutual reliance and respect – partnership – the output is significantly increased.

Flow is both the natural and essential part of all life. The universe around us is in a constant state of flow. Leaves grow on the trees, mature, fall off and become compost, then the cycle begins again with new buds. The oceans ebb and flow. The planets, including the Earth, are in a state of interdependent motion. In the same way, each human being is an embodiment of many systems; we too are in a constant state of flow. We have a cardiovascular and circulatory system that sends blood around the body via the heart, arteries and veins, delivering oxygen and nutrients to organs and cells. We have a digestive and excretory system that provides nutrients for the stomach and intestines and eliminates waste from the body. We have an endocrine system that provides chemical communications throughout the body using hormones. We have an autonomic nervous system (the parasympathetic system and the sympathetic nervous system) that collects and processes information from the senses via nerves and the brain and tells our muscles to contract to create physical actions. We have many more systems, including but not limited to the integumentary system, exocrine system, lymphatic system, immune system, reproductive system and respiratory system.

The circulatory system works in a similar way as the universe. The circulatory system is a closed system; everything that goes out has to come back. The universe works in exactly the same way. The heart is a pump and with every beat of the heart, blood is pushed out to approximately 70 trillion cells and travels approximately 60,000 miles (more than twice around the Earth) before returning to its source. Exactly the same amount of blood that is pushed out returns. If there is a minor block in the system, then high blood pressure results. If there is a serious block, then a heart attack will occur. All ill health essentially arises from an impediment to the natural flow of the systems of the body. It is exactly the same within a business.

It has been suggested that, 150 years ago, 93% of all money in issue was in circulation, whereas now, 92% of all money in issue is not in circulation. If true, this means that only 8% of all money circulates. I have no idea what the criteria for this assertion might have been, but we know that at the height of the recent global financial crisis, the peak of the crisis came when interbank lending dried up. Banks stopped lending to each other and the global financial system would have collapsed if governments – central banks – had not stepped in. The most obvious catalyst of global financial collapse, which could still occur, is a complete lack of liquidity. Flow is essential in the financial system, as with all other systems.

Every business operates in the same way. Where there is optimum flow between the different parts of the business and a dynamic of interdependence is created, the business will thrive. Where there is a lack of flow, and individuals and departments become quite literally stuck in their ways, the business will, sooner or later, fall apart. A major part of Business Alchemy is diagnosing and releasing the blocks within the business. Many of these obstacles are readily identifiable. However, it is important to appreciate that, although there is an awareness of these blocks, they are not being cleared because it would threaten the status quo and hence they are still limiting potential. Other obstacles are less easy to identify and require an exploration of the hidden dynamics of the business.

Within every business there are many different areas of flow that become restricted. At the basic level, all businesses operate within a physical environment. Larger companies spend hundreds of thousands of pounds on external experts to advise them on the optimum ergonomic flow of the physical environment. It is recognized that this is important for efficient functioning of the employees who work there. The physical environment will include elements such as air temperature, lighting and white noise. Recent research has validated the significance of these factors to flow. Daniel Kahneman[13] is an Israeli-American psychologist notable for his work on the psychology of judgment and decision-making, as well as behavioural economics, for which he was awarded the 2002 Nobel Memorial Prize in Economic Sciences, a testament to the boundary-breaking nature of his research. He has consulted with most Fortune 500 companies and written extensively about the effects of the physical environment on decision-making.

Similarly, in the UK, Paul Dolan[14], is a professor of Behavioural Sciences in the Department of Social Policy at the London School of Economics and Political Science and is director of the Executive MSc in Behavioural Science, which began in September 2014. He demonstrates the influence of the office environment on performance. Both Kahneman and Dolan are behavioural scientists who conclude that a substantial amount of decision-making and judgment in the business environment is being made by factors outside the decision-maker's awareness.

For example, a well-known fast food chain established that if all the walls in their retail outlets were painted yellow instead of pink, then customers spent seven to eight minutes less time there and turnover was improved.[15] None of the customers had any awareness that the colour of the walls was affecting and influencing their decision-making. In the same way, it was discovered that patients recovering from surgery recovered between 30% and 35% quicker if a large plant was placed in their room.[16] The existence of a living, breathing organism in their environment significantly aided reparation. None of the patients had any awareness of this. And so it is with business decisions. There are many variables in the environment that are affecting decision-making without the knowledge or awareness of the conscious mind.

In the Eastern tradition, great importance is placed on feng shui[17], the natural flow of energy through a physical space. Feng shui is a system for arranging your surroundings in harmony and balance. In Chinese, the words feng shui literally mean 'wind' and 'water', both of which flow in abundance around the planet. Feng shui is gaining momentum in the corporate environment as employers recognize that obstacles within the physical environment impede performance.[18] Simplistically speaking, it can readily be appreciated that an overcrowded office with bulging filing cabinets, towering piles of papers on desk and extraneous clutter impedes efficient performance. A cluttered physical environment interferes with clarity of thought. At the other end of the spectrum, a well-styled, slick, clean office promotes productivity.

The next level of flow to consider is in the area of communication. Within all organizations there are various types of communication: verbal, nonverbal, e-mail, handwritten, telephone and face-to-face. Each of these vehicles of communication can support the flow of the organization or inhibit it. Jesper Juul is a psychologist who has worked within family systems for more than 30 years and has developed a blueprint for healthy communication within families. Every business is, of course, a family. He talks about values, which could more accurately be described as a set of guiding principles. These guiding principles play an important role as a compass when we enter into conflicts and need to make decisions. If we do not have a set of guiding principles within the relationship, we will move from conflict to conflict and life will be hectic. If you do not have a compass to help you navigate, you could end up exactly where you do not want to be.

Jesper Juul writes about four fundamental values or guiding principles[19]:

1. Equal dignity
2. Authenticity
3. Personal integrity
4. Personal responsibility

Equal dignity is about understanding that everyone's opinion matters. It's being interested, curious and respectful of others, seeing, hearing and valuing them. Authenticity is about being honest in your communication about how you are feeling and expressing what your needs are as clearly as you can. Personal integrity is about defining your boundaries and making choices and decisions that better support yourself and your needs. Personal responsibility encourages taking action that supports your personal integrity and being responsible for your thoughts, emotions, feelings, actions and responses. This approach is not a set formula, but rather something that can adapt to situations as well as personal and cultural styles.

Whatever the position or role an individual has within a business, communicating with an agreed-upon set of principles that assume equality at the human level greatly enhances performance. The CEO and the typist, the leading sales executive and the filing clerk, are all entitled to a set of values, irrespective of their roles.

One may be paid large sums of money to make difficult decisions and guide the direction of the business, while one may be paid a modest amount of money to arrange the files, but the business cannot function without either. By embodying responsibility and authenticity, there is a mutual respect and understanding of each other's importance to the business as a whole. Adapting these values within a business environment – or indeed any set of thoroughly considered values – makes business life much more meaningful, as you avoid working in a chaotic way, shifting from conflict to conflict in constant search of solutions or methods.

A critical element of all communication is the flow of ideas. In a system that relies upon independence and dependence, or superiority and inferiority, the flow of ideas is not encouraged. Within a family, where there is a rigid, all-knowing, all-powerful patriarch or matriarch, everyone else within the system knows that it is not safe to question the explicit or implicit assumptions. The family system becomes an increasingly narrow environment, where no new ideas or alternative positions can be expressed. As the individuals within the system lose their voice, the family as a whole becomes contracted.

In a healthy family, each member is encouraged to have a view. There is an open exchange of ideas, and everyone has their say. It is not that the parents cease to be the parents and children cease to be children. We are not talking about equality of role, but equality of individuals. At the end of the day, when each family member has a voice, it remains up to the parents to make decisions based upon the best interests of the family as a whole. It is exactly the same in any business. It is the responsibility of the chief executive to make decisions. But if decisions are made in isolation, without the benefit of a wide range of views from every level of the organization, it becomes an impoverished decision.

Optimum flow within business is when every level of the organization listens to the other with mutual respect based on an appreciation of partnership. This mutual reliance leads to more intelligent decision-making. It is not cooperative, but it is collaborative. Certain individuals within an organization are paid to make decisions. Flow creates improved decision-making.

Just as we have seen with a family, if the head of the system is rigid and closed, the group will not grow and expand. A key element to flow is the open, expansive strategy of a business. This does not mean that we end up with wishy-washy direction, where anything goes. It is about clarity of thought and focus, which can adapt to a changing environment, both externally and internally, to embrace new ideas as they arise. The word 'solution' has two different meanings. Its original meaning was of a liquid, a homogeneous mixture of two or more substances in which the molecules or atoms of the substances are completely dispersed. A solution flows to where it is needed. The second meaning, which has evolved from the first, is to solve a problem. A problem is a situation where something is stuck and there is an absence of flow. Then there is a need of a solution in the literal sense.

Each business is made up of different departments or teams. In larger businesses, there may be several different corporate entities within the same group. It is difficult to imagine any business without competition between the different areas. Sometimes there is a competitive spirit to produce the greatest amount of revenue each year, the highest profit or greatest number of new clients. A certain amount of competition between the different areas of a business is healthy. Just as within a family, a healthy, natural competition between individual children, and between children and parents, can be enjoyable and fun and create an atmosphere of wellbeing. However, when this competition tips over to being destructive, sometimes based on both conscious and unconscious envy or a desire to belittle the other, it becomes counterproductive and limits the performance of the family or the business. Much of the work of Business Alchemy is about discovering unhealthy and destructive behaviours between different areas of the business, often based on a deep-seated envy or dissatisfaction within the destructive team. The solution starts with helping the parties see that this is limiting them both. Neither team is fulfilling its potential. Moving the teams to a dynamic of partnership helps both areas to expand and opens up to the natural flow of new areas of opportunity.

HOW TO INCREASE FLOW:

1. Discover the blocks inhibiting flow.

2. Create collaboration rather than competition.

3. Have the courage to step into the unknown.

4. Get out of the way.

CHAPTER FOUR

THE
SHADOW

In the previous chapter, we have seen how obstacles and blocks interfere with and impede the natural flow of a business. The shadow is the hidden part of the business: an area largely outside the awareness of the executives of the company. For an individual, the notion of an unconscious block is, indeed, a strange phenomenon. If it is unconscious – outside of awareness – how can we know about it? The history of modern psychology and psychotherapy, starting with neurologist Sigmund Freud[20], has attempted to answer this question. Early solutions for this were dream interpretation, hypnosis and free association.

The best and simplest analogy for this phenomenon is an iceberg. Anyone who has ever seen an iceberg close up will know that the part above the water line is enormous. However, that visible part is small relative to the even larger area unseen beneath the surface. Psychologists and psychotherapists, despite coming from radically different backgrounds and practising very different methods, agree that as human beings we are conscious of only 5% to 10 % of who we are. This means that 90% to 95% of who we are is outside our awareness at any given time. Even at the level of perception, scientists tell us that we have something called a perceptual field, which in every given moment is filtering out a huge amount of information and selecting the preferred data. The criteria for selection of whether data arrives in our awareness or not is multifaceted and multi-layered. A team of researchers at Warwick University concluded that in these times, we receive the same amount of data in each day of our lives that Shakespeare received in his entire lifetime. None of us need reminding of the constant bombardment of data we now receive in modern life. It is little wonder that the bulk of this is sent to the unconscious mind, to be buried in nanoseconds.

Business Alchemy is all about exploring the hidden dynamics of a business – what lies beneath the surface. The focus for most businesses is the visible world. Executives create business plans, financial plans and marketing plans and undertake market research focusing on the goals of the business and product development. However, if the organization looked at the energy flow of the business and discovered what was blocking the business from developing and released that obstacle, the organization would evolve and grow naturally and successfully.

Any executive of a business or organization intuitively knows that there is a great deal going on under the surface of the business. There is much that is not being seen or expressed. However, finding a way to make the latent manifest – to give a voice to the unspoken or to articulate an uneasy feeling – is not so easy for businesspeople.

If we take as an example a marriage or a close relationship, there is at any one time a plethora of issues or dynamics that are going on under the surface that both parties are aware of, but they are not being addressed for a variety of reasons. It is the same with any business. There is a shadow side to all relationships within an organization: between the chief executive and the chairman, the marketing director and the finance director, and the sales manager and the office manager. But in addition to the individual relationships, there is also a shadow side to the business as a whole.

To illustrate the hidden dynamics and how these are exposed through Business Alchemy, we will look at a number of specific examples.

COMPANY A

This successful manufacturing business had created a niche that generated significant opportunity for growth. After several years of increased profitability, the business had suddenly experienced two flat years. While the business remained highly profitable, the ambitions of the key stakeholders were being frustrated. Despite immense drive and energy, the business appeared to be stuck.

I worked with the chairman and chief executive, who were both shareholders in the business. During the second session, an innocent remark about feeling that the company needed to do more in terms of its social and charitable contributions, opened up a whole new arena. What became evident was that the company had fixed ideas of what acceptable success constituted and what excessive success represented. We explored this in terms of the prevailing culture. It was recognized that within the UK environment, a certain amount of success is tolerated, but too much success can be seen as vulgar. It is also perceived to attract envy and attack from others. This UK environment could be compared to other cultures; for example, in the US, there is a gréater tendency towards celebrating success and the view that the greater the success, the better.

In this particular company, we discovered an unconscious embarrassment and awkwardness about being seen as too successful. There was a perception that their success was hurting other companies in the sector, those using old technology. It was important to allow all these beliefs, values and perceptions to be aired without judgment. As we worked through this process, there was a tangible release of new energy to allow the business to reach its full potential. Within months, the business attracted substantial new orders, and there was an exponential growth curve over the next two years.

Just as there are many rings in the trunk of a tree, there are many layers of value embedded in the different groups that constitute our environment. It starts with an individual, expands to a small team, a larger group, the organization, the dominant culture and the global geo-political landscape. Each and every one of these groupings can be affecting the repressed dynamic of an individual and an organization.

One of the outcomes with this business and its executives was that there was a significant shift in perception from believing that their excess success was damaging others, to seeing that their increased success created success for others.

A similar but different block can be seen with the following example of an organization operating in a contrasting arena.

COMPANY B

This organization was a large philanthropic company operating in the area of education, training and change management. The key personnel were highly motivated by integrity and spiritual values. They were focused on aligning the business in all the right ways. However, the business had been stuck for several years, unable to grow and develop. The business was not expanding and new clients were hard to come by. It took several meetings before the core of the problem emerged. Within the individuals and the organization was an unconscious distrust and contempt for money, particularly what they deemed to be excessive wealth. This was the shadow of their philanthropic endeavours.

The more this was explored, the clearer it became that money and profit were seen as 'dirty' and undesirable. Following their initial business success, it was easy to see how the brakes on the business had been applied, based upon these unconscious judgments. We worked on repositioning the value of money, wealth and profit, and the possibilities of expansion for the organization based upon these values. The executive team could readily grasp that the greater the success and profitability, the larger the outreach of their philanthropy. Although the uplift was slow, due to residual resistance, the organization began to expand and grow. Twelve months later, it was performing with substantial increased revenue and profitability.

The same simple principle can be seen to be operating here: i.e., what is outside of awareness and is unconscious is powerful and drives the behaviour – whether of the individual or the group. Once this has been made conscious, there is a process during which old beliefs and judgments are transformed to create a new constellation of values aligned to the new vision. Individuals and groups carry systems of old beliefs that are buried and yet create a significant effect on the business. In large businesses, it becomes essential to look at the explicit and implicit core values of the organization.

The next example comes from a much smaller commercial organization founded as a family business.

COMPANY C

This was an SME business originally founded by an innovative and powerful married couple. When I was working with them, there were a number of external shareholders. The company had succeeded in driving revenue at a compound rate of 30% per annum over six years and yet remained unprofitable. This created a great deal of tension within the organization.

At our first meeting, it quickly emerged that the dynamic between the married couple, who were chairman and chief executive, was seriously inhibiting the market opportunity and profitability of the business. There had been several attempts to align with private equity to greatly enhance the business and take it to the next level. On each occasion, the particular deal had fallen through at the last moment.

When we worked with the key personnel, after some resistance they saw that there was a massive conscious and unconscious fear of losing control of the business and not wanting to 'lose their baby'. Interestingly, as is often the case, the course that they were set on was guaranteed to achieve precisely that. By highlighting the various ways in which this destructive fear was operating, the executives were able to acknowledge that they were creating the very outcome that they most feared.

Over the course of the next three months, by bringing these various unconscious fears into awareness, the individuals and company were able to move beyond this. The business rapidly became profitable and developed a number of completely new international markets. As part of this process, we supported a reorganization of the board, which allowed for better communication and flow at the top of the organization.

It is true in many different contexts that holding on tightly or seeking to control outcomes severely inhibits and restricts the natural flow of abundance and achieves the one thing that we want to avoid. Energetically, it is the opposite of trust and optimism. Businesses that are overly cautious often create a limiting and constricting environment that suppresses the natural creativity within the organization. Opening to unknown potential and opportunity often feels risky, but it is a crucial part of having faith in the creative essence of the organization.

COMPANY D

The next example concerns a highly successful company of international management consultants that called me in as part of an annual routine assessment and enhancement of the business. There was no specific problem to address. As part of my preparation for the first day with this client, which was to involve 35 of their senior partners, I spent 40 minutes engaging with their website. The standout feature for me was the extreme emphasis on integrity and any value aligned with authenticity. It felt to me that this was unnecessarily exaggerated. I decided to spend the day exploring where the partners individually, and where the company as a whole, were being inauthentic and fake with their clients. The immediate reaction to this was not promising. I asked the assembled group, many of whom were Oxbridge graduates, how many were married or in committed partnerships. More than 80% of those present raised their hands. So I then posed the question of how many of them were, on a regular basis, inauthentic or fake in this relationship. Every hand shot up. I expressed incredulity that they could acknowledge being inauthentic with their beloved, but never with their clients. It took several hours of painstakingly leading this group through different exercises before it became self-evident to everyone present that of course, from time to time, individual executives and the company as a whole were inauthentic or fake with a client. For this particular business, this was a major breakthrough and an important realization. They began to see that the overemphasis on integrity and authenticity was a compensation for not being able to tolerate the possibility of being insincere, inauthentic or fake.

This dynamic can be easily seen in the identity and behaviour of individuals. If you take an individual of fundamentalist religious persuasion, the one characteristic that they cannot tolerate is doubt. So they have to assert certainty, over and over again, to eliminate all possibility of doubt. This leads to a narrow and restricted world view, with serious consequences for action and behaviour. Much of our individual, personal development work and our corporate coaching and leadership programmes have an underlying foundation and tendency to affirm the positive. This can be helpful up to a point, but invariably becomes counterproductive. It is exactly the same with any business or organization. If we desire more integrity, then we achieve this by bringing awareness to where we are being inauthentic. If we desire more honesty, then we do this through bringing awareness to our dishonesty – not by seeking to convince ourselves and others just how honest we are.

The shadow of any organization often contains the opposite polarity of the corporate identity that has been created and is being massaged on a daily basis. What lies beneath the surface is more powerful and dangerous than bringing it into consciousness. This is well illustrated with the final example.

COMPANY E

This privately owned estate agent had been struggling to stay afloat for several years. The owner/manager of the business, despite having made severe reductions, was not able to cover his monthly living costs. At our initial meeting, it was revealed that several years earlier this business had operated as a 50:50 partnership between the existing principal and his friend and colleague. A conflict had arisen that resulted in the other party leaving the business under acrimonious circumstances.

After a short exploration, we discovered that while consciously the main protagonist was desperately trying to build a successful business to prove a point to his ex-partner, unconsciously he was furiously aggrieved at the way he had been treated. He was more determined to hold onto the grievance than to create a successful business. This perverse dynamic is all too common in individuals and organizations. We worked with the individual and the company to release and let go of the grievance and to wish the ex-partner well. Once this energetic block had been released, the business slowly but consistently commenced an uplift in performance and profitability.

It is important to understand that both individuals and companies can be consciously completely committed to a particular course of events, while outside of their awareness, there are other unconscious forces consistently undermining and sabotaging the stated objectives. This is true of all areas in life; what is unconscious (outside of our immediate awareness) is always more powerful and is often running and ruining our lives. Making the unconscious conscious dissipates and punctures these unwelcome blocks to success.

HOW TO EXPOSE THE SHADOW:

1. Accept that there is an unseen world outside of our awareness.

2. Be prepared to loosen your grip on identity.

3. Allow the unconscious to become conscious and take ownership in yourself of what you are judging in your colleagues.

4. Take a risk to try something different.

CHAPTER FIVE

THE
INNER
AND
OUTER

The vast majority of us live our working and domestic lives as if the outer world is primary. This is the dominant zeitgeist in the Western world and in most other cultures – but interestingly, not in all cultures. We spend our lives being busy with the outer world, the external world around us. We focus on our jobs, relationships, homes, cars and holidays. We spend our time rearranging the furniture of the outer world. We change jobs, we change relationships, we move house, we upgrade our car in the belief that it will makes us happy, that it will change how we feel inside. One of the core principles of Business Alchemy is that the outer world is in fact a reflection of our inner world. We live in a holographic universe. This view of the world has existed for thousands of years among most indigenous cultures; e.g., Maoris, Native Americans and Aboriginals. The community most recently adopting this view of the world can be found within quantum physics.

In 1935, an Austrian physicist, Erwin Schrödinger, famously created a thought experiment, now widely understood and accepted within the scientific community, which has become known as 'Schrödinger's Cat'[21]. Schrödinger created a scenario in which a theoretical cat was put in an enclosed box. Inside there was a bowl of food that was covered, and the lid needed to be released before the food could be consumed. The box was then covered for a period of days, beyond which the cat could not survive without food. At the quantum level, the cat was both alive and dead at the same time – both possibilities existed. Schrödinger argued that when an observer returned to the box to remove the cover, whether the cat was alive and hence had discovered how to remove the lid and eat the food, or whether he was dead and had not discovered how to eat the food, depended upon the intention of the observer at the time of removing the cover. It was not, in any way, dependent on whether the cat had discovered how to get the food.

In the decades that followed, many scientists, including the physicist David Bohm[22], the neurophysiologist Karl Pribram and Michael Talbot, who researched quantum mechanics, have all independently reached the conclusion that the universe operates on a holographic model. This model suggests that reality as we experience it isn't real, but merely a projection of consciousness – our inner reality. This view is also embodied in many modern-day Hollywood blockbusters, including *The Matrix* and *Inception*.

In 1982, at the University of Paris, a research team led by physicist Alain Aspect performed what many people have referred to as one of the most important experiments of the 20th century.[23] Aspect's team discovered that, under certain circumstances, subatomic particles such as electrons are able to communicate instantaneously with each other, irrespective of the distance separating them. It does not matter whether the particles are ten feet or ten billion miles apart. Somehow each particle always seemed to know what the other was doing. This research contradicts Einstein's long-held premise that no communication could travel faster than the speed of light.[24] David Bohn, probably the most significant theoretical physicist of the 20th century, maintains that Aspect's findings show that objective reality doesn't exist – it is simply a projection of our inner consciousness.[25]

These ideas might seem confusing and irrelevant to the average businessman and woman going to work each day and playing their part in increasing their company's revenue and profit. However, if true in whole or part, this has radical consequences for the way in which we live our lives and run our businesses. Given the far-reaching implications of this, surely it behoves us to at least consider and open the door to this possibility? I readily acknowledge that embracing such a massive shift in perception is a leap akin to the Copernican Revolution. Prior to the 16th century, everybody living on the Earth 'knew' that the sun revolved around the Earth.[26] The Earth was the centre of our universe. The more educated and the more intellectual you were, the more you affirmed this view. It was the prevailing belief and so to question it would have seemed insane. Yet this is precisely what happened when the Prussian astronomer and mathematician, Nicolaus Copernicus, came along and suggested that the Earth moved around the sun. The academics and intellectuals of the day dismissed him as mad.

This shift in awareness that Copernicus was seeking to introduce took well over 100 years to be acknowledged and accepted as true. The Catholic Church convicted Galileo of suspicion of heresy for promoting Copernicus' view in 1633, and did not drop its opposition to heliocentricity (a system that refers to the sun being at the centre of the solar system) until 1835. Protestants were still opposed to this view during the 17th century, though by 1609 Johannes Kepler had firmly supported heliocentricity.[27] It was not until Newton showed *why* the planets move around the sun (gravity) in his *Principia*, published in 1686, that heliocentricity became firmly established. Copernicus was in fact correct and everyone else wrong. What had once been thought to be unthinkable was now the dominant world view.[28]

While this shift in the primacy of the inner or outer world might seem ridiculous to ordinary people, there are in fact many entry points that demonstrate this reality in everyday life. For example, we have created completely different cultures across the planet: e.g., Iran, China, Norway and Japan. But if we ask any police officer in any of these countries, they will tell us that if 20 people witness a car accident 15 metres away, they see a different car accident and the differences that they witness are substantial. Some see a red car. Some see a green car. Some see a female driver. Some see a male driver. It is well documented that the witnesses of a car accident often have ferocious arguments defending their position. The truth is that there really were 20 different car accidents.

In exactly the same way, if there is a major argument in the middle of an office, the individuals who witness it will all report it differently because what they see is governed by their internal filters. Every human being has been conditioned in different ways – within family systems, culture, religion and education. It is through this filter that we see and create our reality on the outside. Three people or 30 people witnessing a woman speaking loudly to a small group of men will experience this completely differently. Some will report that the woman was aggressive, while others will say that she was amazingly empowered. Some will be inspired by the experience, others highly critical.

At first sight, the idea that the outer world is a reflection of our inner world might appear ludicrous. However, following a basic enquiry of certain daily experiences, this might become more understandable.

In the previous chapter, we saw how an unconscious embarrassment and awkwardness around being seen as too successful limited the growth of Company A. In

Company B, we saw that unconscious negative judgments about money and profit were responsible for the underperformance of the business. In Company C, the tremendous fear, both conscious and unconscious, of losing control of the business created the very outcome that was most dreaded. In Company D, the corporate identity that could not allow the possibility of inauthenticity or fakeness was beginning to slow down the growth record of the business. And finally, in Company E, a deep unconscious grievance, completely outside of awareness, was repeatedly bringing the business to the brink of collapse.

In each case, the internal world, which was largely hidden, was creating the outer reality of the business. The more we open our minds to this possibility and test the data empirically, we begin to learn that it cannot be otherwise – this is how the world works. The whole nature of the relationship between the inner and the outer world can be understood through the dynamic of cause and effect.

In everyday life, we use the expressions 'what you sow is what you reap' and 'what goes around comes around'. This is closely linked to the Eastern idea of karma. In our business lives, as well as our personal lives, we spend our time and energy focusing on what 'comes around', i.e., the results of our actions. There is a profound insanity about this, because we are creating the circumstances in the outer world and then trying to control what cannot be otherwise.

This can readily be seen in the manager in an office who is constantly creating drama and conflict, only to spend all their time and energy putting out the fires that they themselves created. They are oblivious to this, but if they stopped and paused for a moment and could see that they are creating the outer situation every day, then they could refocus their attention on creating a different outer reality through adjustment to the source.

Just as the directors and employees of an organization spend their time and energy focused on the dynamics of the outer world, so do the vast majority of coaches and consultants engaged by businesses to support performance. The terms of engagement adopted take place within this predominant world view. Business Alchemy does not and will not engage with a business at this level because experience has taught me that it has limited value. Rather, we are focused on the inner world of the individual executives and the business as a whole. What does this mean? All human beings have volition and will. Earlier, we referred to the work of Daniel Kahneman, a Nobel Prize winner in economic sciences for his work on the psychology of judgment and decision-making, and Paul Dolan, professor of Behavioural Sciences in the Department of Social Policy at the London School of Economics, who have shown that in a business environment, a large percentage of decisions and judgments are made for reasons outside of the awareness of the decision maker.

The business itself has a corporate identity of which it is conscious, and there are a multitude of factors operating within the business outside this narrow identity. The difficulty for individuals and organizations is that will and volition (and, as we will see shortly, intention) operate at both the conscious and unconscious level. It is the unconscious element that is limiting and, in some cases, operating in a destructive manner. Individuals and businesses often spend their entire lives operating with a conscious strategy, clearly articulated, while at the same time unconsciously undermining their best efforts and ensuring that they do not achieve their stated goals.

Business Alchemy works on this vast, less tangible area beneath the surface. The focus of all my work is on the intention of the business and the key executives, because it is the intention that creates the outer world. Rather than concentrating on what has already been created, i.e., the manifest, all of our attention is on what is doing the creating, i.e., the latent. By paying attention to restrictions and blocks in the inner world, which are unseen, it releases reserves of creative energy that enhance outer-world performance.

HOW TO CREATE OUTER WORLD SUCCESS:

1. Open to the possibility that the outer world is a reflection of the inner world.

2. Allocate space and time to explore the inner dynamics of the business.

3. Recognize in business discussions that we each have our own filter and projector.

4. Commit to challenging and changing what is behind the projector.

CHAPTER SIX

INTENTION

One of the most underrated powers in the universe is intention. Nothing in the universe exists without intention. The house you live in, the car you drive, the clothes you wear, the relationships in your life and your favourite music cannot exist without intention. In fact, even you do not exist without intention. At the heart of every business, every strategy, every marketing initiative, every client interaction, is intention. However, the power and reality of intention is regularly misunderstood and rarely harnessed.

Intention is the creative power that fulfils our dreams – whether they are about money, relationships, love, material success, spiritual awakening or sporting achievement. An intention is an inner impulse, which is focused in a particular direction and contains within it the seed of that which you seek to create. Just like real seeds, intentions can grow or perish according to the richness of the soil and the attention they receive. All too often, our intentions are cast into fallow ground to wither and die. This leaves us with a feeling of futility. Equally, sometimes our seeds of intention exist on mediocre soil, where the roots are not strong, so the fruit or the flower is disappointing. Occasionally, the seed of our intention falls on fertile soil and bears fruit in abundance.

In addition to the quality of the soil (the environment), all seeds need sunlight and water in the right proportion. And they need attention. Every business operates in precisely this way. For a business to exist, one or more people created an intention that then became a reality. Many businesses struggle in less than optimum climates while others seem to prosper exponentially. In my experience, there is nothing more important than intention in determining the success or failure of a business or the level of success a business achieves. This principle applies in the same way to an individual's life. The majority of time and energy that we spend in our business life is dominated by thoughts, emotions, reactions and firefighting, which eventually becomes its own consuming routine. There is very little room for reflecting upon intention.

In many businesses, time is set aside once a year to leave the office environment and spend one or more days in a country hotel to discuss strategy and direction. However, even then it is often the case that the intention for this quality time is dominated by familiar, well-worn agendas. The first and most important criteria for creating an intention that will fulfil the potential for the business and the individuals who make up the business is providing some space and stillness in which clarity becomes possible. In the first chapter, we talked about the principle of simplicity and how this enables clarity, which creates a new pathway ahead. If our intention is too choked up with explicit and implicit agendas, it becomes self-defeating. The seed has not taken root.

When we create space away from the office to have a profitable discussion that creates clarity of vision and thought, all too often a return to the office environment, with the demands of daily life, dissipates the power of the intention. The business returns to its default setting of not fulfilling its potential. This is despite the appearance that every effort is being made to align with the intention. The seed has not received appropriate levels of attention.

It is important for us to distinguish between intention and desire. Every day, numerous desires arise. We may desire a cup of tea or desire some fresh air. Desires are similar to feelings. They are intransient and can fall away as quickly as they arise. One moment we can feel greatly aggrieved by something, and shortly afterwards we may feel deep appreciation. In contrast, intention carries the power of creativity and, if properly cared for, is enduring and steadfast.

Every business, wherever it is on the spectrum of success, can achieve a significant uplift through the power of intention. A critical element in the offering of Business Alchemy is spending a day on resetting the intention of the business. As we have seen above, the prerequisite for this is creating space away from the endless daily demands of e-mails, text messages, phone calls, meetings and client conferences. Time and again, during a session on intention I have witnessed key executives being distracted by texts, e-mails and messages on their mobile phones. This inability to allow space and to be truly present to the discussion has been magnified through the advent of mobile phones. This level of distraction and avoidance is often hidden under the mantra 'the client is king'. Executives see themselves as being at the beck and call of major customers. However, if care and attention is not being given to the business (and of course, to the executives themselves), then the business stops serving its customers in an optimum way. In the procurement process, it is astonishing how difficult it is to get a group of executives to agree to a few hours away from their immersion in the business. Without creating quality space, the process is undermined.

Whether sitting with two or twenty executives, it is a wonderful process to begin to explore the true intention of a business. One can only do this with a spirit of openness and curiosity. If we start such a process thinking we know the answer already, it will have limited value. Through this process, there is always a great deal of energy released in individuals and in the group. It is almost as if you can see the obstacles and blocks choking the true intention release their hold. It is like a weeding process. This takes time and is particularly nuanced. The skill is in not rushing and pausing to listen within. At the end of the day, there is always an immense clarity of intention. It is also fascinating how, in my experience, there is never disagreement or conflict once the true intention has been articulated. Rather, there is a sense of renewed unity and a bond between colleagues around this intention.

When we discover or recreate the true intention of a business, it often consists of a number of different components. For example, when working with a large public relations company recently, the intention statement we arrived at was: "To restore deep connections through fully integrated communication, while having fun and creating financial value of £100 million." It can immediately be seen that this intention is made up of four separate but interrelated components:

1. Restoring deep connections
2. Ensuring fully integrated communication
3. Having fun
4. Creating financial value of £100 million

When working with companies, particularly those in the UK, it is interesting how often it is the intention to make money that is the most difficult to articulate, including putting a specific figure on the intention. It is very important when creating an intention to be specific. For example, if we simply create an intention to create money, what does that really mean? The answer is that it means radically different amounts to different people, whereas if we create an intention to make

£10 million, everybody (including the universe) knows what we mean.

Intention, while sharing many similarities with the idea of a mission statement, is not the same thing. A mission statement can be imbued with intention or not. It can be creatively guiding a business and informing all important business decisions, but as we are all too well aware, this is rarely the case. Intention carries within it the DNA of the business. DNA (deoxyribonucleic acid) is a molecule that carries the genetic instructions used in the growth, development, functioning and reproduction of all known living organisms. This is precisely how intention works within the business, starting with an idea by one or more people to becoming a global multinational business such as Apple or Amazon.

The thing that most people struggle with over intention is the contrast and differential between the conscious and unconscious spheres. People develop a strong conscious intention that is constantly being undermined by what is below the surface: their unconscious intention. An individual may have a conscious intention to have a relationship, so joins dating sites and goes to parties, yet never meets the right partner. They blame circumstances and complain all the time. The real reason they remain single is that there is an unconscious intention, which is stronger, that is ensuring that a relationship does not occur. Why? In this example, every time they have been in a relationship previously, they were badly hurt and heartbroken. This unconscious intention overrides their conscious intention. In the same way, a business might constantly affirm and reaffirm the need to double its revenue and profit. It creates five-year business plans that demonstrate this conscious intention, yet it never comes to fruition. The business again blames external factors: currency fluctuations, Brexit and American elections. The deeper truth is that there is a stronger, unconscious intention to maintain the status quo because of myriad fears around greater success: the fear of attack, envy and the potentially destructive nature of too much money or power.

Once the business has unearthed and exposed the unconscious blocks to its intention, I always suggest that the final, clear intention that has been articulated is put on the website and discussed at every client meeting. This elicits a range of reactions, from mild discomfort to hysterical panic. We have entered the second part of the process. It is interesting how many businesses are embarrassed about telling clients or potential customers that they want to make a lot of money or that one of their key drivers is that they want to have fun. All these objections are a crucial way of seeing how we dilute and limit our intention. It is an important part of the process to witness first-hand what is getting in the way of the intention. There is little point in creating an intention if we then water it down or keep it hidden in discussion with key stakeholders. For an intention to be powerful, we need to be able to stand proud in the energy of that intention and quite literally shout it from the rooftops. It is not, in fact, essential or critical to put our intention on the website or to voice it in every client meeting. The reaction to this suggestion demonstrates the value in the process. However, it can readily be seen that if, when pitching to a major new client, you can incorporate the intention of the business within the pitch, you are literally giving life to the seed of that intention.

What we need to do is embody the essence of our intention. Once the executives have seen the ways in which the intention is undermined, my next request is that the intention is written out on a sheet of paper and laminated. Then I ask that every executive stand on this piece of paper for a minimum of two minutes every day. They quite literally step into the energy or essence of the intention. The reason why this is both important and powerful is that it is an extraordinarily simple way of embodying the intention in every cell of the body. Of course, the mind throws up objections and scepticism, but I always explain that this is entirely empirical. Do it and see if it works. It is surprising how many executives find this exercise on intention leaving them full of enthusiasm, yet they never carry this out. The reasons for this failure vary. Some individuals find it embarrassing, some have already decided it is pointless (they know better), while others may have decided that they don't have time. It is astonishing that if you ask people to commit two minutes out of every 24-hour period, they are unwilling to make this commitment. If you really wanted to change your business, surely, even the greatest sceptic could commit two minutes from a place of curiosity to discover whether this works or not?

I recently worked with a company in the hedge fund industry. Following a day on intention, there was a tremendous sense of excitement and enthusiasm for the newly articulated intention. There was no embarrassment about making plenty of money, yet on the three-month check in, out of a team of six executives, not one of them had stood onto their laminated intention sheet for one day. We had a follow-up meeting two months later and eventually, I persuaded them, as an experiment, for everyone to do this for a period of 30 days. The results were evident to the team: four significant business acquisitions and an overall increase in funds under management were achieved in the following two months, with a resultant increase in the bottom line. A number of the team remained highly sceptical and found it difficult to believe that this simple process of standing on a piece of paper could have affected the outcome. My response is always that it doesn't matter if the entire team remains sceptical if the desired outcome has been achieved.

Having created the seed of intention, it is important to follow it up with an appropriate amount of daylight, water and attention. If you neglect it, it will wither and die. The next aspect of intention is the difference between rigidity and worry at one end of the spectrum, and flexibility and trust at the other. As individuals and as organizations, sometimes we create an intention and immediately form a rigid attachment to both the intention and a specific outcome. The attachment arises from a fear and insecurity that the outcome will not happen, rather than a deep trust in the process. The fear and insecurity create the exact outcome we are seeking to avoid. Similarly, we often spend our days compulsively worrying and thinking about the intention, often convincing ourselves that we are nurturing and nourishing the seed of the intention. This is erroneous and misguided. It will always result in the opposite of what we most want to create. Once we have clearly articulated the intention for our business, we need to harness the creative power of this through a small amount of daily homework and then let go in the spirit of trust.

Letting go is connected with trusting that the intention will reach its fulfilment. At one end of the scale, we can neglect our intention completely, and it will fail to manifest. At the other end of the scale, we constantly agitate and worry about the outcome, which equally destroys the potential. It's like an unexpected monsoon that washes the seed away. The optimum way is to maintain focus in a spirit of trust: knowing that the intention will bear fruit from its own innate intelligence. I often ask the question, "Does an acorn know what it is to be an oak tree?" The truth is that an acorn has never seen an oak tree and cannot possibly know what an oak tree is. However, with the correct amount of sunlight and watering, over time the oak tree appears and thrives. In this sense, the acorn knows exactly how to become an oak tree. It contains everything it needs to know to fulfil its potential. It is precisely the same with every business. Fortunately, this happens a lot quicker than it takes for an oak tree to flourish.

The final piece of the role of intention is recognizing that we do not have to do it all ourselves. We exist in a culture that is driven by doing and making increasing amounts of effort. Even though we all know when we pass the point of no return, where greater collective effort yields less reward, we continue to work longer hours in more frenetic office environments. Once we truly understand the nature and power of intention, we are able to harness the infinite power of the universe itself. We plant our intention, provide it with an appropriate amount of nourishment and trust (i.e., knowing) that it will reach its fulfilment without our constant interference.

HOW TO CREATE INTENTION:

1. Brainstorm with your team, allowing ideas, however wacky, to be voiced.

2. Keep refining the words until there is resonance within.

3. Articulate it in a clear sentence.

4. Physically step into the energy of the intention every day.

CHAPTER SEVEN

ALIGNMENT

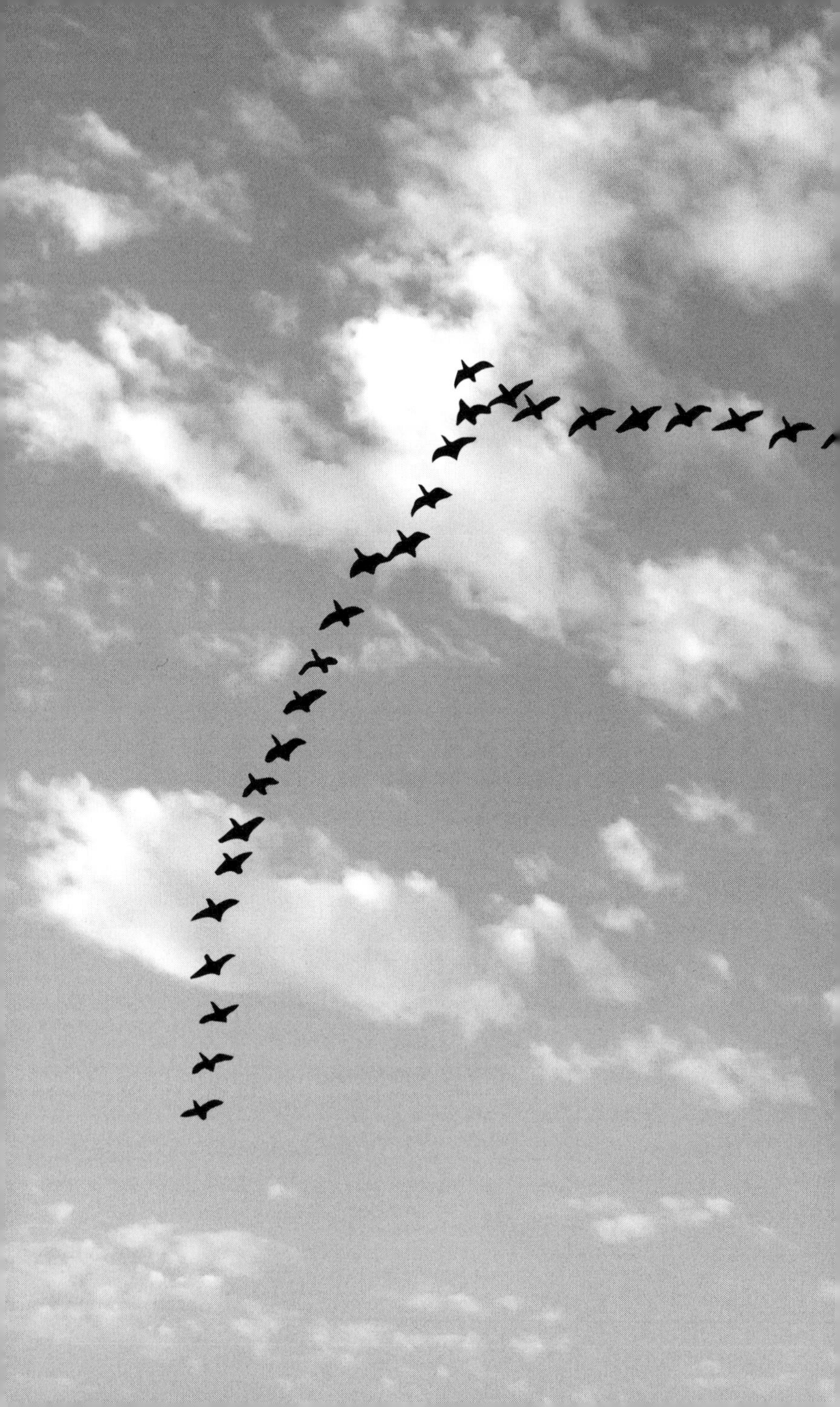

We saw in the last chapter how the best-articulated intentions can evaporate and disappear through the frenetic environment of business life. If intention, which is one of the most powerful creative forces in the universe, is to be effective, we must find ways of supporting it. The first step is to embody the intention, through stepping into the essence of the intention on a daily basis. It is important to fully understand the need for alignment in the body.

The human body has approximately 75 trillion cells. It is difficult for the human mind to imagine one trillion, let alone 75 trillion cells. According to Dr Deepak Chopra[29], every cell in our body has a higher purpose, insofar as 'it is interested in the whole' rather than the individual. The cells in the stomach are not only thinking about the stomach, but are also digesting food, supporting the brain and the functioning of the body as a whole. Equally, the cells in the brain are not only thinking about the brain, but about coordinating the legs and arms, as well as many other processes in the body. In addition to being interested in the whole, every cell operates through the principle of efficiency, i.e., 'do less and accomplish more'.

Every cell is extremely adept at giving and receiving from other cells. They naturally create an environment of interdependency. We saw in Chapter One that most human beings and businesses oscillate between dependency and independence, yet all too rarely achieve an environment of interdependency, which is optimum for the business. Over the past 12 months, I have sat with more than 30 CEOs, and at some point in the conversation, as casually as possible, I have suggested that if they themselves spent 30% less time in their business and encouraged their entire staff to do the same, then it is probable that their revenue and profit (and other KPIs) would increase. The surprising and shocking aspect of this is that not one of these chief executives disagreed. In fact, they all nodded in the affirmative.

The truth is that not one of them knows how to implement this or if they did, have the courage to do so. Optimum output is based on interdependency, not on more effort. The cells of our body know this innately and intuitively. Businesses achieve interdependency through recognizing the critical importance of each individual and each department within the organization. Each one of the 75 trillion cells in our body contains the totality of who we are. There is a particular view, developed from the work of Dr Deepak Chopra, which recognizes that every cell has the memory of wholeness. When we lose that memory of wholeness, whether as an individual, a business or a single cell, we have a disease. A cancer cell is simply a cell that has lost its memory of wholeness – the cell is operating on an 'only for me' basis. In this state of selfishness, it starts to destroy the body. Its integrity and existence is interdependent upon every other cell in the body, but it does not recognize this. It pursues its own agenda to the cost and detriment of the whole.

It is precisely the same with an individual and a business. Imagine a top sporting team, a premier-league football team. Consider one of the players working for his own glorification rather than the benefit of the team. It becomes destructive. It is corrosive within the team and factions are created. If each member of the team is focused on the whole as the higher purpose, the team will consistently outperform. Whereas the moment any one individual forgets the memory of the whole and focuses on the 'me', it undermines the output. Every successful sporting manager knows this. It is exactly the same in every business.

Once the individual executives have embodied the intention of the business, it is vital to create alignment within the board of directors. Anyone who has ever served as a director on the board of a limited company will know that, invariably, one or more directors are acting unilaterally, which undermines the direction and performance of the business. Worse still, there are often factions within a board pulling in different directions. The individual directors are operating from independence, with no sense of interdependency. They have lost the memory of the whole – the greater potential of the business – and are acting like rogue cancer cells. Until the board of directors is united behind the spirit of the intention, there is little point in turning up to work each day.

Having achieved alignment within the board, it is critical to instil the stated intention within the next layer of management. This involves a similar procedure as with the board. Each individual needs to embrace and embody the essence of the intention for the business. The procedure of alignment is for the intention to cascade down through every level of the organization, from the boardroom to the post room. Some areas of the business might be more resistant and throw up greater obstacles than others. However, it is crucial for *all* parts of the organization to be singing from the same hymn sheet. It is necessary to spend as much time as required to get all individuals and departments within the business to sign on to the intention in the spirit of interdependency. In exactly the same way, when an individual decides to walk across the room, every cell in the body is aligned with that intention.

In the process of embedding the intention throughout the organization, it is important to recognize that it is the responsibility of the board of directors to create and set the intention, not the sales department or the marketing or finance departments. As the intention is imbued into the various parts of the organization, it is not up for debate. It is predetermined by the board. If certain key individuals do not feel able or willing to align with the intention, it is critical that they leave the organization at this point. This is healthier for the business and the individual, rather than remaining in the environment and undermining the strategic direction of the business. Too many businesses cling on to a high-performing individual or division that is rowing its own boat, in the mistaken belief that the business will not thrive without them. Actually that individual or division becomes like a cancer cell, eating away at the body of the business.

This process is in alignment with the guiding principle of simplicity outlined in Chapter One. Decisions might not be easy, but they are always simple. Is the individual or the department fully aligned with the intention or not? When embedding the intention into different areas of the business, it is appropriate to allow discussion and debate and allow all views to be aired. At the end of the day, though, the seed of the intention has been planted, and anyone or anything that does not support the development of this seed needs to be pruned for the health of the organization. Pruning always creates a more abundant harvest.

The intention of the business becomes the guiding principle for every internal and external business discussion. When considering a significant collaboration with a third party or with a new client group, the overriding consideration should always be, "Does this align with the company's intention?" It is better to make the hard but simple decisions at this point than to store up trouble for the organization down the road. Too many businesses make decisions to expand in a way that is not aligned with the intention or the purpose of the organization. This is another way in which the intention is diluted and undermined. This further underlines that the principles of simplicity and flow operate in an elegant way. The decisions to be made might not be easy, but they are always simple.

In the previous chapter, we used the example of a business whose intention statement was 'to restore deep connections through fully integrated communication and having fun while creating a financial of a £100 million'. Let us suppose a major organization is discussing transferring their business to this company and that this organization would become one of their top three clients. It is easy to understand how much effort and enthusiasm would be directed to winning this account. However, at various stages, different members of the new business team voice concerns about the natural fit of this client with their business. This particular public relations company is only interested in promoting an organization with substance over style. They need to know that their clients are delivering value to their customer base.

The new business proposition is more interested in style over substance. They require massive self-promotion without really delivering on their promises. In this example, the seduction of short-term reward is allowed to override the deeper awareness being expressed by members of the new business team, that this is not in alignment with the intention of the company. It can be readily seen how, over time, the lack of authenticity and integrity in the client company will rub up against the public relations company to create conflict and discord that will have a detrimental effect on the whole. It is always better to make the difficult but simple decision at the outset rather than to pay the price later, which may include risk of damage to reputation, deterring other clients from engaging, and creating internal divisions and conflict among key executives internally.

The need for alignment is far wider than the business environment itself. A theme running through Western civilization is the paired concept of the macrocosm and the microcosm. This view was most fully developed by the early Greek philosophers, especially Plato, who espoused this view in *Timaeus*. It is the view that human beings (microcosm) parallel the whole universe (macrocosm) and vice versa. This view is known as 'the macrocosm is the microcosm'. The origins of these words are *kosmos*, which means order or the ordered world, and has come to mean the universe or cosmos[30]. Macro means large and micro small. It arises from the observation that there is a similarity in pattern, nature and structure between human beings and the universe. This approach contains within it the idea that the microcosm contains the memory of the whole, just as the individual cell carries the memory of the whole.

Within sociology, it is an accepted form of enquiry to study a small group of individuals, whose behaviour is then seen to be the same as a much larger social body. Within a business environment, it is frequently profitable to study the dynamics within one division or one group company as a way of providing insight into the dynamics of the business as a whole. Vital lessons can be learned for what remedial action may be required in the organization to bring this back into alignment.

The organization as a whole aligns with the intention based upon the following three assumptions:

1. The whole is greater than the sum of the parts.
2. Every cell (department or individual in the organization) has a memory of the whole.
3. Interdependency (not dependency or independence) creates the principle of efficiency: 'do less and accomplish more'.

Ultimately, once we align our business with its intention, we are bringing the business into alignment with the wider environment, the macrocosm. Just as we saw with intention itself towards the end of the last chapter, rather than working harder and harder with increasing effort, we align our intention and tap into and align with the organizing infinite power of the universe itself. We plant our intention and provide it with an appropriate amount of nourishment and trust via alignment in the knowledge that it will reach its fulfilment without our constant interference; just as the acorn one day becomes a magnificent oak.

HOW TO ACHIEVE ALIGNMENT:

1. Create board unity behind
the intention.

2. Ensure the intention is embodied
through every layer of the business.

3. Display the intention internally
and externally.

4. Trust that this outcome will
be achieved.

CHAPTER EIGHT

SYNCHRONICITY
SYNCHRONICITY
SYNCHRONICITY
SYNCHRONICITY
SYNCHRONICITY
SYNCHRONICITY
SYNCHRONICITY

Synchronicity is a concept first introduced by psychoanalyst Carl Jung[31]. It maintains that events are 'meaningful coincidences' if they occur with no causal relationship yet seem to be meaningfully related. Jung's theory of synchronicity was in many ways the culmination of his lifelong engagement with the human condition and expresses the view that the structure of reality includes a principle of acausal connection, which manifests itself in the form of meaningful coincidences.

This theory has been developed further by Dr Deepak Chopra, who coined the term synchroDestiny, which he defines as: "When you consciously manifest your destiny through intention, using the phenomenon of synchronicity or meaningful correspondence or meaningful coincidence."

In Chapter Five, we looked at the relationship between the outer world and the inner world and suggested that the former was a reflection or manifestation of the latter. As we saw, the physicist Alan Aspect discovered that subatomic particles are able instantaneously to communicate with each other, irrespective of the distance separating them. It does not matter whether the particles are two feet or twenty billion miles apart. Somehow each particle always seemed to know what the other was doing. This research contradicted Einstein's long-held premise that no communication can travel faster than the speed of light. David Bohn maintains that Aspect's findings show that objective reality doesn't exist – it is simply a projection of our inner consciousness.[32]

In earlier chapters, we have looked at the need for simplicity, the nature of flow, the importance of clearing the blocks and obstacles, the critical role of intention and the significance of alignment. When all these factors are addressed, synchronicity occurs with spectacular results. The concept of synchronicity contains two separate but related theories.

The first aspect depends on our understanding of the relationship between the inner world and the outer world. Once we fully appreciate that we are the projector creating our external reality, then we begin to see how external reality can be reorganized and changed to suit our goals. The most telling analogy is the example of an individual sitting in a cinema watching the film of their life. At some point, they reach a part that they do not like, and they walk out of the cinema, get into their car and drive to another town. They walk into a different cinema, expecting to see a different film. It is the same film. They leave the cinema, drive to an airport, get on an aeroplane, arrive at another country, and walk into a cinema, convinced a different film will be showing. It is the same film. This is how we are living our personal and business lives.

In my 20s, I fell in love with Australia. I visited the country two or three times every year for several years and seriously considered emigrating. At that time I remember saying to a number of friends, "There is one fundamental flaw with Australia: I take myself with me." As individuals and as businesses, we spend our lives rearranging the furniture of the outer world, constantly surprised that the overall outcome never changes. As an individual, we leave one relationship and start another with someone who seems completely different, only to discover that the same dynamic arises. We leave one business and start another business, where similar issues arise. It is not until we shift our attention to the inner world, behind the projector, that we can create meaningful change. If the images behind the projector change, then the outer world will automatically alter in a corresponding way. This is why the nature and role of intention is so important. It can readily be seen that the image behind the projector and the image on the screen have to be the same. Hence, they are synchronistic. We live our daily lives, managing our businesses, consistently referring to situations as coincidences or accidents or random events. We live our lives as if we are at the mercy of external forces – when in fact we are creating our reality every day.

The second aspect of synchronicity relates to the theory that when we are in alignment with our purpose and intention, the universe aligns with us. What does this mean? The universe is full of innate intelligence. Nature is replete with examples of different species acting with a collective memory; for example, a massive shoal of fish changing direction as if it were one, or a colony of termites acting with one collective intent.

Last year, when visiting the Serengeti, I learned that when a family of giraffes is chomping off the Acacia tree, when they are about halfway through, the tree emits a pheromone that is particularly distasteful to giraffes. They move on, allowing the tree to regenerate. However, it is not only this tree that emits a pheromone; it acts as a catalyst to other trees within a certain radius, which simultaneously emit the same pheromone, resulting in the giraffes moving on to a different area. The trees communicate with each other.

Rupert Sheldrake, a Cambridge biochemistry don and Harvard scholar and a leading Darwinian, introduced the term 'morphic resonance' as a process whereby self-organizing systems inherit a memory from previous similar systems.[33] Sheldrake's morphic resonance hypothesis posits that 'memory is inherent in nature' and that 'natural systems, such as termite colonies, or pigeons, or orchid plants, or insulin molecules, inherit a collective memory from all previous things of their kind'. Morphic resonance means that the so-called laws of nature are more like habits. This leads to a radically new interpretation of memory storage in the brain and of biological inheritance. There is a shared reality into which we can all connect or disconnect at any time. When we are clear about the seed of our intention and it is aligned with our purpose, the universe joins us in this enterprise. If we plant a seed and tend the soil, the wider environment provides the sunlight and the rain. Today we have a business culture that is driven, requiring more and more effort, and longer working hours, in the mistaken belief that wilfulness will get us where we want to be. Although hard work and effort are necessary and to be valued, the obsessive and compulsive nature of this is counterproductive. If instead we sat back, relaxed and gave our attention to the inner world, the desired outcome would be far more effective. Everything that we see in the outer world has its roots in the hidden world. The beauty of synchronicity is that it works as a constant biofeedback mechanism, giving us valuable data as to how we need to adjust our inner signal on a daily basis. Intention is rather like the old-fashioned radio valve that sends a signal out into space and by turning a dial you eventually tune into the required transmission. What arises in the outer world is constantly reflecting our inner hidden intentions. If, based on this information, we retune our intention, we will create a different outcome.

As uncomfortable or bizarre as this might seem to many businesspeople, it is testable through empirical experience. I witness this happening on a daily basis with companies that engage with Business Alchemy. In Chapter Four we discussed the privately owned estate agent that consistently held an unconscious major grievance against his ex-business partner. The trading of his business was consistently reflecting this. Once we cleared the hidden resentment and reset the intention, the business began to prosper. Equally, in the example of the profitable manufacturing business, there was an unconscious block to being seen as too successful. The synchronicity in the outer world was reflecting this hidden inner intention and obliging the company with acceptable but uninspiring results. Once we cleared this inner obstacle, the business was significantly propelled forward.

For business executives whose whole conditioning and training has been based in outer-world strategy, techniques, tools and formulae, it does require a Copernican shift to be willing to turn their attention to the inner world, and the hidden blocks and obstacles contained therein. However, a small amount of openness goes a long way. Any business that is willing to explore these possibilities witnesses the efficacy and results, but more importantly, begins to open to a new arena of potential.

At one end of the spectrum there are many academics, scientists and left-brain-dominated rationalists who see life as a series of random acts and coincidences that are in no need of explanation. Implicit in this world view is the idea that life happens to us. It rains, earthquakes occur and burglars break into our homes and steal our prized possessions – randomly. At the other end of the scale, there are many more right-brain-dominated artists, innovators and those strongly led by their intuition who do not believe there is any such thing as coincidence, and recognize that life is embedded with meaning. In fact, there are scientists and deeply religious individuals at both ends of the spectrum. In both cases there is a tendency to defend the dogma at all cost. My request to businesses is to be open to enquiry with a sense of curiosity. In a practical, everyday sense, most people have an experience of synchronicity. You bump into someone in the supermarket who has been on your mind for three days, whom you haven't seen for six years. You go to phone an old friend, only to find that the phone is ringing – it is your friend on the line. Travelling through a remote airport, you bump into an old school friend you haven't seen for decades.

An exploration of these phenomena, and manifesting more of them in your life leads to personal fulfilment and increased business opportunity. For example, you fly to New York and a senior executive of the company best placed to acquire your business is sitting in the next seat on the plane. The truth is that we can significantly influence and multiply these so-called coincidences.

HOW TO SUPPORT SYNCHRONICITY:

1. Recognize your role in creating your outer reality.

2. Understand that what is happening around you is your most valuable teacher.

3. Recognize that an important part of your intention is outside of your awareness.

4. Reset your conscious and unconscious intentions.

CHAPTER NINE

NOT
KNOWING

As we discussed in an earlier chapter, in Sanskrit, one of the oldest languages on the planet, there are two principles, Ra and Ma. Ra is the masculine principle and Ma is the feminine principle. Rationality is derived from Ra, while magic is born from Ma. Today, our business culture, as well as the wider culture, is significantly out of balance with too much Ra and not enough Ma – we need more magic. Within Ancient Greek culture, often described as the origin of Western Civilization[34], there are two types of knowing. The first, *episteme*, is the most established form of knowledge, i.e., knowing facts and information about the world. It is where we get the branch of philosophy known as Epistemology. The second, *nous*, is more akin to an intuitive knowing and is where we get the word nous, which means common sense. Business Alchemy is more attuned to the latter.

In the *Road To Larissa*[35] , Plato expands this distinction in knowing through an enduring example. He sets out a position whereby an individual could study a map of the road to Larissa (a city in ancient Greece) over and over again, to become familiar with every nook, cranny and turn in the road. In this sense, it could be said that he completely knows the road to Larissa. This is contrasted with an individual who has physically walked every step of the road to Larissa. In the latter, there is an intimate experience of the journey, which the first 'knower' can never attain. A modern example of Plato's distinction is that if someone turned up from another planet and wanted to know about love, you could give them the ten best books ever written about love. They could read each book three times over and the question would still remain: "Do they know anything about love". Until one has had the experience of falling in love, with all its excitement, nuance and pain, it can never really be claimed that you know about love.

The business world is dominated by rationality, theory and strategy, and light on intuition. However, every successful businessperson, in my experience, is highly intuitive without necessarily recognizing this particular strength. Successful people tend to listen to their gut instinct and their intuition.

All change, transformation and magic arise from not knowing. However, we tend to live our lives from a place of knowing. For example, if we attend a talk or seminar on how to be a successful entrepreneur, we sit there thinking, 'he's got that right', 'he hasn't fully understood that', or 'he's wrong about that'. We evaluate the talk against what we think we already know. If we review our daily lives, most of our time is spent evaluating our experiences against what we think we already know. This position, by definition, excludes the possibility for new knowledge. It is restrictive and narrow, rather than expansive and creative. One of the reasons for this approach, as we saw in an earlier chapter, is that the brain is essentially a pattern-recognition pro-gramme, always seeking the familiar.

Interestingly, even in the most rational, logical, analyti-cal community in the world – the scientific community – many of the most important breakthroughs and discov-eries come when the team of scientists is exhausted and has hit dead end after dead end. They reach that point of giving up and sitting back in the not knowing, and a moment of inspiration arises. This is the Archimedes experience. The Archimedes moment occurred because he suddenly realized that an observation, apparently quite unrelated to what he had been intending to solve, actually provided the answer – a moment of '*nous*' or intuition. Isaac Newton's moment of inspiration, when he saw the apple falling off a tree, is similar. Some might argue that Einstein hit on the theory of relativity by sit-ting in a train and watching a train on the adjacent plat-form moving in the opposite direction; again, a moment of intuition. Certainly, "To grapple with a problem that has eluded all who have come before, to explain a part of the world in a novel way with clarity and logic, requires not merely a great deal of thought and experimentation, but also a flash of insight, a moment of creativity. It is in that sense that the search for inspiration is common to scientists and artists."[36]

Within Business Alchemy, whether I am working with an individual or a group of executives, I am constantly putting myself into a place of not knowing. This has taken several decades of practice and development, but I have discovered time and again that in this place of not knowing, inspiration and completely new ways of knowing arise. I have also discovered that this is entirely reliable. Steven de Souza and Diana Renner have written a book on this topic, *Not Knowing*, which became the bestselling management book of the year. The subtitle of the book is: "The art of turning uncertainty into opportunity."

De Souza and Renner argue that, "By developing a unique relationship with not knowing, we discover a new way of living, working and succeeding in our modern world." As a white Caucasian male, all my life I have been exposed to the pressure to know. As a young boy, I remember well inventing answers rather than admitting, "I don't know." I discovered later that by throwing in a few key expressions, such as 'research indicates' or '83% of people agree', that it is possible to sound authoritative and knowledgeable rather than admit not knowing, which is unreasonably humiliating. I can still find myself proceeding down this path on automatic pilot, despite several decades of fighting against it. The pressure to know in a business environment is incredibly strong. We need to cultivate a culture where the expression "I don't know" or "I have absolutely no idea" is both acceptable and engenders curiosity. Over the past decade, I have met a large number of highly intelligent and accomplished men and women who are at the top of their game. I am always surprised by how often I hear them saying these expressions or similar with ease.

It takes a certain level of confidence in one's self and one's knowledge to be able to articulate not knowing. Whereas always thinking that we know stems from a particularly unhelpful arrogance, which is a compensation for insecurity.

Another aspect of knowing and not knowing, which is critical to understand, is the distinction between control and trust. We are all aware of Sir Francis Bacon's famous phrase, "knowledge is power",[37] but the compulsion to know is usually based around the desire to control. We can look at this historically, with obvious examples found in the church and religion. We can also look at this through our individual lives, where anxiety arises at the thought of not being in control. The opposite of control is a simple trust or faith in what will happen. The truth is that none of us know what will happen in the future. Yet we spend huge amounts of energy trying to predict and control the future.

As we have already seen, the best way to ensure a successful outcome is to give attention to the inner world, particularly intention. There are clear examples in the world where an emphasis on knowledge leads to

certainty and the expulsion of doubt. Increasing attention and energy is given to affirming the knowledge.
The one thing that cannot be entertained is doubt.
This is particularly true in the religious arena, but also
applies to the political arena and in much of business
life. A little-known psychologist called Gordon Allport
said, "All faith is fashioned in the workshop of doubt."[38]
There is tremendous wisdom in this statement, yet it is
now largely countercultural. The way to develop more
trust in our working lives and in our environments is
to entertain and befriend doubt, not to keep affirming
the increasingly restrictive certainty that we are right.
The latter leads to a shrinking business and ultimately to its own demise. Another element of doubt over
knowledge is that it encourages curiosity, creativity,
humour and play – all of which are in short supply in
the business world.

De Sousa and Renner maintain that, "When we reach
the edge of our knowledge, our default responses include
clinging to our existing knowledge, attempting quick-fix
solutions or avoiding the situation altogether."[39]

How do we encourage and give permission for not
knowing to flourish within a business setting? The best
motivator is to witness the power of not knowing and
the efficacy of the results. As with everything else, culture is best shaped from the top. It needs to start with
the CEO and the board of directors. If the CEO is an

all-knowing, my-way-or-the-highway individual, there is little hope of ever facilitating an environment that nurtures not knowing within the organization. CEOs are paid a great deal of money to make decisions. If they are operating from an all-knowing platform without a healthy proportion of not knowing, they are literally firing on two cylinders. They are limited in their leadership. It is unthinkable that a CEO would address all employees or the company's annual general meeting and adopt the position of not knowing. Similarly, no politician or head of state would address the electorate from a place of not knowing. However, this would be an immensely powerful experience, particularly because it is aligned with the truth. We are probably some way off from this happening within a major corporation. All CEOs can model the truth of not knowing in business discussions, and formal meetings including board meetings, where they explicitly and implicitly give colleagues permission to do the same. When a group of executives are willing to sit in the place of collective not knowing over a particular issue, clarity and inspiration arises.

Another area where this is particularly powerful is with executives who are in front of clients. In most businesses in which I have experience, it is unthinkable for an executive pitching to a new client or holding a key meeting with an existing client to admit that they do not know an answer to the client's need. When executives have the courage and willingness to sit in this place of not knowing with clients, it is not only reassuring to the client (all clients experience within themselves not knowing on a daily basis), but it leads to a much more creative and effective outcome.

Recently, when I was coaching a CEO of a large property company, he was initially nervous and resistant to this idea. Although sceptical, he agreed to experiment with this concept. The day after our session, he had an extremely important pitch to a larger competitor. In the middle of this meeting, he found himself spontaneously admitting that he had no idea in relation to a critical issue. He later told me that he felt incredibly empowered in the meeting, and that he was subsequently amazed by the reaction of his audience. This led to a collaboration that significantly changed the size of his revenue overnight. An important element of the power in the practice of admitting not knowing is its relationship to authenticity and truth. Individuals, whether potential customers or colleagues, respond extremely well to authenticity. They are attracted by and drawn to the essence of truth. Equally, we are all becoming increasingly repelled by the levels of inauthenticity in our business communities, politics and wider cultures.

In our business day, we need to create space and stillness, where we can allow a sense of not knowing. In this space of not knowing, a new kind of knowing can emerge. Once we are prepared to step into the arena of not knowing, it is full of previously unrealized potential. In Ancient Greek philosophy, Aristotle was the first to write about the distinction between potentiality and actuality. He concluded that potentiality is far more potent than actuality because once something has been actualized, it instantaneously becomes limited, as all other possibilities fall away. While potential remains, there is a wide variety of possibility. Similarly, in Eastern tradition, Buddhist philosophers maintain that nothing is more fundamental than something. They point out that everything arises from nothing. In the state of latency (which is unmanifest), there is a huge creative potency of what is possible. In exactly the same way, a state of not knowing is infinitely more powerful than a state of knowing.

Businessmen and women regularly fear that not knowing will lead to apathy, inactivity and underperformance. They are driven by increased activity and busyness. The power of not knowing is that it always leads to a new way of knowing. It is never the case that we get stuck in an abyss of not knowing. What we are seeking to address here is the great imbalance between knowing and not knowing. We are not trying to eliminate or reject knowing, but to introduce and encourage a proportionate amount of not knowing alongside the knowing. Not knowing will open up creativity, a much wider range of possibility and will achieve an increasingly balanced organization that is more expansive and successful.

HOW TO SUPPORT NOT KNOWING:

1. Step back and create space.

2. Practise saying, "I do not know" in business meetings.

3. Develop a realization that there is significantly more that you do not know than you do know.

4. Learn to trust your inner truth.

CHAPTER TEN

ALCHEMY

The core of Business Alchemy is the realm of what is possible. Alchemy owes its roots to the medieval quest for the elixir of life, based on an ability to turn base metals to gold. Alchemy is both philosophy and an ancient practice focused on achieving transformation and transmutation, leading to wisdom and inner freedom. Business Alchemy is not primarily concerned with coaching senior executives, leadership or fixing rogue parts of a business. Rather, it is focused on achieving fundamental transformation within the organization itself.

The modern-day base metal in business is frenetic activity, macho competitiveness, diminishment and disempowerment, mediocrity, political correctness, inauthenticity, compulsive thinking, addiction to worry and anxiety, the need to complain, an addiction to being offended, a lack of purpose and a lack of fulfilment. The transformation possible is into a way of being and working more precious than gold. It offers a sense of purpose and meaning, collaboration and connection, fulfilment, success and recognition, a sense of authenticity, achieving career dreams and actualizing new levels of potential.

As we have seen, instead of focusing on the outer machinations of the business, Business Alchemy explores the hidden internal dynamics. These are inhibiting the best efforts of the board of directors and staff to move the organization forward. By unearthing and diagnosing these blocks, the energy will be released and the strategic direction of the business will flow in accordance with desired goals, outcomes and profitability. All human beings and all businesses limit their potential with a series of largely unrecognized limited beliefs. A limiting belief is something that constrains us in some way. We have limiting beliefs about our identity, both our individual identity and our corporate identity. We also have limiting beliefs about other people, organizations and the world around us. The two simplest and best examples of limiting beliefs are 'I can't' and 'I don't know how'. I often give executives the homework of spending one day listening to how many times they hear the expression 'can't' in business meetings and also within their own internal and external dialogue. There are not too many guarantees in life, but every time we say "I can't", we are guaranteed to stay where we are.

In more than 90% of cases where we say "I can't" it is really a substitute for the truth, which is that "I won't" or "I don't want to". The list of things that we cannot do as individuals or as a business is much shorter than we would like to think. We spend our working lives constantly limiting what is possible in a myriad of different ways without really taking stock of what we are doing. It is rather like we are in a hypnotic state, consistently limiting what is possible, while at the same time giving the responsibility to someone or something else

–complaining about something outside ourselves, other individuals, the business or wider geopolitical events. Business Alchemy is about shifting from a constrained, restrictive view of the world to an open world with infinite possibility. It is about taking responsibility for the environment that we create.

The second most limiting belief, in my experience, is 'I don't know how'. Similar to 'I can't', this is also guaranteed to keep us stuck. In my work with businesses, I regularly encounter people saying, "We want to change this", or "we want to change that", but "we don't know how". This is a deception and a delusion, for the fact is that they do not want to make this change because the familiar is too comfortable. To say "I don't know how" has become a convenient cop-out.

The list of limiting beliefs is endless and would include 'I do', 'I don't', 'I am' or 'I am not'. We often define ourselves by what we do or do not do. For example: I am a salesperson, so I do not do administration. I am an artist, I am not a financial expert. Equally, there are a long list of 'should' and 'shouldn'ts' based on values, cultural norms, laws and other rules that constrain what we should and shouldn't do. We may choose to retain some of these 'shoulds', but in every case it is helpful and beneficial to change 'I should' or 'I shouldn't' to 'I choose to' or 'I choose not to'. In this way, it becomes expansive rather than limiting. For example, rather than saying, "I shouldn't rubbish my competitors", which always feels like I am being denied something, we can reframe this as, "I chose not to rubbish my competitors" (because to do so will have negative effects on myself and my business). In this way, something negative and restrictive has become positive and expansive.

While many limiting beliefs relate to ourselves and our business, we also have limiting beliefs about other people and the world in general. For example, we might regularly think that other people are not reliable or that other people cannot be trusted or that other people are superior or that other people are selfish. Similarly, we have limiting beliefs about the world and life in general. Our starting point might be common limiting beliefs, such as 'bad things happen', 'life is out to get you', 'success never lasts' or 'life is unfair'. Imagine what your professional or personal life would look like if your expectation or belief was that whatever occurs is positive and for your overall benefit. Even temporary setbacks would turn out to be optimum.

When I reflect on what the dominant energy running the planet might be, I get a strong sense that it is lack. We run our lives and we run our businesses on the basic assumption 'there is not enough'. We are always looking for more and we have created cultures that are addicted to more. These cultures are similar to an individual addict who can never get enough and is relentlessly seeking the next fix. Capitalism and most of the structures that we have created are embedded in this foundation. Competition is seen as necessary and highly desirable. What if every morning when we arrived at our place of business, there was an inner knowing that there is enough: enough of everything. There are enough clients, money, revenue, profit and hours in the day. The truth, which might be unpalatable to many, is that if we start our day or run our business with the assumption or belief that there is not enough, then it is certainly true that there will not be. Equally, if we start our day or run our business from the belief or assumption that there is enough, there most definitely will be.

This takes us back to one of the key principles in Business Alchemy: we create our outer world from our inner world. We are the projector. Just as in Erwin Schrödinger's example, whether the cat is alive or not, depends on the thought of the observer. This change in perception requires a Copernican shift. Schrödinger's work is largely accepted within the scientific community, but when we come to embody this in our everyday life and our business life, we recoil in horror. It feels antithetical to everything we think we know and countercultural to common sense.

We are living at a time where there is an epidemic of disconnection. Individuals and communities feel disconnected from themselves and others. Hundreds of millions of people are disconnected via prescribed medication, hundreds of millions more through excess alcohol and recreational drugs. Significantly more than through drugs and alcohol are those disconnected through pornography, while many more disconnect themselves through Facebook, overeating and exercise – the list is endless. During my lifetime, we have created the internet, which now appears to connect several billion people; however, my sense is that overall this has in fact created greater disconnection.

The fundamental truth about the universe is that everything is connected. We are living at a time when science and spirituality are converging to demonstrate this simple pervading truth. The cosmic absurdity is that from this place of interconnectivity, we have created cultures with an all-pervasive level of disconnection. Scientists refer to the El Niño effect;[40] El Niño is a climate cycle in the Pacific Ocean with a global impact of weather patterns. The suggestion is that a butterfly in one part of the world flaps its wings and eventually, the consequences are felt on the other side of the planet. Every mystic from wide-ranging traditions reports the same underlying reality: that everything is one. Indigenous people of different traditions maintain the same truth. Carl Jung, a contemporary of Sigmund Freud's, coined the term 'collective unconscious' to refer to structures of the unconscious mind that are shared and common among all beings of the same species. The collective unconscious is populated by instincts and archetypes, universal symbols that all human beings recognise.

In Chapter Eight, we noted the work of Rupert Sheldrake, who introduced the terms 'morphic fields' and 'morphic resonance', which lead to a vision of a living, developing universe with its own inherent memory. Sheldrake has conducted many experiments that show that dogs know when their owners are coming home, or more importantly, when they decide to come home, a significant time before their arrival. The history of physics has been about exploring deeper levels of reality. For several centuries, Newtonian physics dominated, until eventually this was seen to have a major limitation insofar as it did not explain the atom. A whole new language, theory and science was needed and developed to understand atoms and the nature of subatomic particles – this gave birth to Quantum Mechanics. Atoms and particles function in a radically different way to everyday objects. As we have seen, following Aspect's work in 1982, early Quantum Mechanics was not capable of explaining Einstein's theory of relativity, insofar as it found that particles do travel faster than the speed of light. This led to the Quantum Field Theory.

Dr John Hagelin is a renowned quantum physicist and scientist with a PhD from Harvard. Hagelin conducted pioneering research at CERN (The European Centre for Particle Physics) and at the Stanford Linear Accelerator Centre.[41] He is responsible for the development of a highly successful grand unified field theory based on the superstring – a theory that was featured in a cover story of the scientific magazine *Discover*. There are, in fact, a number of different superstring theories, but each one shares the idea that superstrings are rather like rubber bands, in that they vibrate at different frequencies. Hagelin refers to quantum field theory as 'extraordinary', 'staggering' and 'mind blowing'. In his opinion, "It fulfilled Einstein's lifelong quest to discover the unified source of the diverse universe and discovered the fountainhead of nature's intelligence." Quantum Field Theory suggests that underneath everything is an ocean of pure existence or pure abstract intelligence. It is not dead, but teeming with unmanifest energy. Physicists argue about the consequences of Quantum Field Theory and many disagree with Hagelin.

Prior to this discovery, we operated with the idea that there was gravitation (a field of gravity), a photon (a particle of light) and particles like the electron and quarks, which was 'rather a hodgepodge in an arbitrary world'. Hagelin discovered that the frequency/vibration within superstring theory would correspond to the ordinary things in nature. From this discovery, it is argued that: "Superstring theory explains all those particles as the inevitable predicted consequence of the unified field in its natural state of vibration". In other words, the outer world is predictable in terms of frequency/vibration. As physicists have known for a long time, the so-called material universe is not material at all. Many physicists take a contrary view to Hagelin, some even dismissing him as very wide off the mark, just as was done with Nicolaus Copernicus several centuries ago. Creating a major shift in perception takes time to assimilate and integrate. According to Max Planck, a highly respected physicist, "Science cannot solve the ultimate mystery of nature. And that is because, in the last analysis, we ourselves are part of nature and therefore part of the mystery that we are trying to solve"[42].

From a completely different perspective, research has been undertaken with individuals who are meditating. Meditation is about going within to experience deeper levels of the mind and to rest in pure being. Under prolonged periods of meditation, the brain develops completely different and unrelated patterns of neurons firing. The patterns are totally different to any brain pattern experienced while waking, sleeping, under hypnosis or drug-induced states, including anaesthesia. In our everyday lives, we regard this inner world (consciousness) as 'subjective' and the outer world (material) as 'objective'. The development of physics from Schrödinger through Quantum Mechanics to Quantum Field theory, along with research of the inner world, through meditation and other altered states, leads to the same truth. Ultimately, the subject, the object and the observing are all one. They are not three separate things. Synchronicity occurs and often appears like alchemy – magic – but the reality is that it cannot be otherwise because the inner and outer are one of the same. This is to fully understand the nature of synchronicity. We have come full circle to the ultimate simplicity of all that is.

In all my work with organizations, I start from the basic assumption that every business is simple. However much the executives and senior management try to complicate the nature of the business or the nature of a problem, Business Alchemy always starts with a return to simplicity. From the reality of simplicity we have seen the importance of flow. Everything from the largest galaxy to the smallest subatomic particle is in a state of flow. Every business is made up of different constituent parts and the flow between them and the entity as a whole supports the outcome. We all know the experience of feeling that our business is in flow; the phone rings with exciting offers, documents are effortlessly written, meetings yield creative results. The feeling of flow is tangible. This is the natural state of being. This, therefore, involves the necessity of removing blocks and obstacles that inhibit the natural flow of the business. A great deal of the work of Business Alchemy is focused on dissolving blocks that are restricting the direction, revenue and profit of the business.

The main driver and creator of flow is intention. The importance of creating clarity and accuracy around intention cannot be overstated. Intention is the compass for the business. Once we have established the pure intention of the business, we can turn attention to creating alignment through the organization. This process naturally leads to synchronicity because the outer reality will automatically match the inner reality that we have created. The seed of intention has been set in motion.

The world of physics, with atoms and subatomic particles, is anathema to those of us living ordinary lives with ordinary things. We see a table or a chair, not a whirling vortex of neutrons, protons or electrons. Similarly, the principles of Business Alchemy can seem foreign and far removed from the successful running of a day-to-day business. However, a limited degree of willingness to open the door to a new way of understanding the nature of the business, and its success or failure, will create an alchemic shift that will reap significant rewards.

CHAPTER TEN – ALCHEMY

RESOURCES

Allport, Gordon (1961) *Pattern and Growth in Personality*
Harcourt College Publishing ISBN 0-03-010810-1

Bohm, David (1995) *The Undivided Universe*
Routledge ISBN 041512185X

Bohm, David (2002) *Wholeness and the Implicate Order*
Routledge ISBN 0415289793

Bohm, David (2003) *The Essential David Bohm*
Routledge ISBN 0415261740

Chisolm, Hugh, ed. (1922). *"Rubicon" Encyclopedia Britannica (11th ed.).*
Cambridge University Press ISBN: 1-59339-292-3

Chopra, Dr Deepak (1989) *Quantum Healing*
New York: Bantam Books ISBN: 0-553-05368-X

Chopra, Dr Deepak (1994) *The Seven Spiritual Laws of Success*
Amber Allen Publishing and New World Library ISBN
1-878424-11-4

Chopra, Dr Deepak (2005) *Synchrodestiny: Harnessing the Infinite Power of Coincidence to Create Miracles*
Rider ISBN 1844132196

Chopra, Dr Deepak (2008) *The Soul of Leadership*
New York: Harmony Books ISBN:0-307-40806-X

Cook, Blanche Wiesen (1999) *Eleanor Roosevelt, Vol. 2: 1933-1938*
Viking ISBN: 0-670-80486-X

Dolan, Paul (2014) *Happiness by Design: Change What You Do, Not How You Think*
New York: Hudson Street Press ISBN 9781594632433

Dolan, Paul (2015) *Happiness by Design: Finding Pleasure and Purpose in Everyday Life*
Penguin: ISBN 0141977531

Drake, Stillman (1957) *The Discoveries and Opinions of Galileo*
First Anchor Books ISBN 0-385-09239-3

D'Souza, Steven and Renner, Diana (2014) *Not Knowing: The Art of Turning Uncertainty into Possibility*
LID Publishing ASIN B00ZY818Z2

Ellwood, Robert and Alles, Gregory (2007) *The Encyclopedia of World Religions*
Facts on File ISBN: 978-0-8160-6141-9

Fendall, Arthur (2010) *All Things Natural: Ficino on Plato's Timeaus*
Shepheard-Walwyn (Publishers) Ltd ISBN 0856832588

Fogelin, Robert J (2004) *The Cambridge Companion to Quine*
Cambridge University Press ISBN: 0521639492

Forman, Lillian E (2010) *Albert Einstein: Physicist and Genius*
Abdo Publishing Company ISBN: 1604538805

Gorbachev, Mikhail Sergeevich (1996) *Memoirs*
Doubleday ISBN: 9780385480192

Jeal, Tim (2011) *Explorers of the Nile*
Yale University Press ISBN: 9780300187397

Juul, Jesper (2001) *Your Competent Child – Towards New Basic Values for the Family*
Straus & Giroux, N.Y. ISBN 0-374-52790-3

Kahneman, D., Diener, E., & Schwarz, N. (Eds.). (1999).
Wellbeing: The Foundations of Hedonic Psychology.
New York: Russell Sage Foundation. ISBN-10: 0871544237

Kahneman, Daniel (2012) *Thinking, Fast and Slow*
Penguin: ISBN 0141033576

Kahneman, Daniel and Tversky, (2000) *Choices, Values and Frames*
Cambridge University Press: ISBN 0521627494

Kalckar, Jorgen ed (2008) *Volume 6 Foundations of Quantum
Physics I (1926-1932)*
Niels Bohr Collected Works. Amsterdam: Elsevier.
ISBN: 978-0-444-53286-2

Kalckar, Jorgen ed (2008) *Volume 7 Foundations of Quantum
Physics I (1926-1932)*
Niels Bohr Collected Works. Amsterdam: Elsevier.
ISBN: 978-0-444-53286-2

Kuhn, Thomas S (1957) *The Capernican Revolution*
Harvard University Press ISBN 0-674-17103-9

Pais, Abraham (1982) *Subtle Is the Lord: The Science and the
Life of Albert Einstein*
Oxford University Press ISBN: 978-0-19-853907-0

Pasternak, Charles (2004) *Quest: The Essence of Humanity*
John Wiley & Sons ISBN 0470851457

Planck, Max (1993) *A Survey of Physical Theory*
Dover Publications ISBN 0486678679

Planck, Max (2016) *The Origin and Development of the
Quantum Theory*
Forgotten Books ISBN 1440037841

Pribram, Karl H. (1991) *Brain and Perception: Holonomy and Structure in Figural Processing*
Psychology Press ISBN-10 0898599954

Pribram, Karl H. (2013) *The Form Within*
Prospecta Press ISBN-10: 193521280X

Quine, Willard Van Orman (1951) *Two Dogmas of Empiricism*
The Philosophical Review 60: 20-43

Quine, Willard Van Orman (1977) *Ontological Relativity and Other Essays*
Columbia University Press ISBN: 0231083572

Russell, Jeffrey Burton (1991) *Inventing the Flat Earth: Columbus and modern historians*
New York: Praeger ISBN: 0-275-95904-X

Sober, Elliott (2015) O*ckham's Razor: A User's Manual*
Cambridge University Press ISBN: 1107692539

Talbot, Michael (1996) *The Holographic Universe*
HarperCollins ISBN-10: 0586091718

Talbot, Michael (2010) *Part 1 Complete – Synchronicity and the Holographic Universe – Thinking Allowed*
Uploaded on Dec 18, 2010 http://www.thinkingallowed.com/2mtalb

Wilber, Ken (2001) *A Theory of Everything*
Gateway ASIN: B00EKYERIS

Wilber, Ken (1993) *The Spectrum of Consciousness*
Quest Books ISBN: 0835606953

BIBLIOGRAPHY

CHAPTER ONE

1   Joshi, Nikul. Sanskrit Definition. Ancient *History Encyclopedia*, 22 August, 2016, https://www.ancient.eu/Sanskrit/

2   Plutarch, *Life of Pompey*, 60.2.9, Perseus Digital Library Suet. Jul 32 http://www.perseus.tufts.edu/hopper/text?doc=Perseus%3Atext%3A1999.02.0061%3Alife%3D-jul.%3Achapter%3D32

3   Johnson, Boris. "The day Churchill Saved Britain from the Nazis" *Daily Telegraph*, 13 October, 2014, http://www.telegraph.co.uk/history/world-war-two/11157482/The-day-Churchill-saved-Britain-from-the-Nazis.html

4   Hirshfeld, Alan, "Archimedes: The Original Naked Scientist." *The Naked Scientists*, 10 October, 2010, https://www.thenakedscientists.com/articles/features/archimedes-original-naked-scientist

5   Gidadhubli, R.G. *Economic and Political Weekly.* 2 May, 1987 http://www.jstor.org/stable/4376986

6   Aristotle. *Metaphysics.* Book H 1045a 8-10
    Oxford University Press
    "… *the totality is not, as it were, a mere heap, but the whole is something besides the parts …* ", i.e., the whole is other than the sum of the parts

7   Mercedez-Benz S Class https://www.mercedes-benz.co.uk/content/unitedkingdom/mpc/mpc_unitedkingdom_website/en/home_mpc/passengercars.html

CHAPTER TWO

[8] Baker, Alan. Simplicity, *Stanford Encyclopedia of Philosophy 29 October 2004*, 20 December 2016
https://plato.stanford.edu/entries/simplicity/

[9] *The Basics of Philosophy: William of Ockham*
http://www.philosophybasics.com/philosophers_ockham.html

[10] Quine, W.V. (1948). "On What There Is" *The Review of Metaphysics*, Vol 2, No. 5 September 1948 *Philosophy Education Society Inc*
http://www.jstor.org/stable/20123117

[11] Newton, Isaac. (1687) *Mathematical Principles of Natural Philosophy*. This translation of the third law and the commentary following it can be found in the "Principia" on page 20 of volume 1 of the 1729 translation

[12] Encyclopedia Britannica, 11th Edition, Volume 15. *Karma meaning deed or action; in addition, it also has philosophical and technical meaning, denoting a person's deeds as determining his future lot.*

CHAPTER THREE

[13] Kahneman, Daniel. Daniel Kahneman - Biographical. *Nobelprize.org*. Nobel Media AB 2014. Web. 23 Jan 2017.
http://www.nobelprize.org/nobel_prizes/economic-sciences/laureates/2002/kahneman-bio.html

[14] Dolan, Professor Paul, Behavioural Science and Director of the Executive MSc Behavioural Science September 2016
http://www.lse.ac.uk/DPBS/About-Us/faculty/paul_dolan/Home.aspx

[15] Haller, Karen Colour and Design Consultancy. *Branding – Why Red and Yellow Are Used by the Fast Food Industry.* 30 March 2011
http://karenhaller.co.uk/blog/branding-why-red-yellow-is-used-by-the-fast-food-industry/

[16] Nardozzi, Charlie. *Plants Help People in Hospitals Heal Faster,* The National Gardening Association Learning Library
11 February 2009
https://garden.org/learn/articles/view/3115/

[17] Field, Stephen L. *The Zangshu, or Book of Burial by Guo Pu.* Translated 26 July, 2009
http://fengshuigate.com/zangshu.html

[18] Levin, Dan. *China Officials Seek Career Shortcut with Feng Shui.* 10 May, 2013 *The New York Times*
http://www.nytimes.com/2013/05/11/world/asia/feng-shui-grows-in-china-as-officials-seek-success.html

[19] Juul, Jesper. *Our 4 Key Values: Adapting these Values.* 18 December, 2013
http://www.family-lab.com/about/our-values

CHAPTER FOUR

[20] Biography.com Editors *Sigmund Freud Biography.* 2 August, 2016
http://www.biography.com/people/sigmund-freud-9302400

CHAPTER FIVE

[21] Merz, Theo. *Schrödinger's Cat Explained.* 12 August, 2013 *The Telegraph*

http://www.telegraph.co.uk/technology/google/google-doodle/10237347/Schrödingers-Cat-explained.html

[22] Haselhurst, Geoff. *David Bohm ... and The Holographic Universe*. SpaceAndMotion January 2005 http://www.bibliotecapleyades.net/ciencia/ciencia_holouniverse04.htm

[23] International Balzan Prize Foundation. *Alain Aspect – France – 2013 Balan Prize for Quantum Information Processing and Communications.* http://www.balzan.org/en/prizewinners/alain-aspect

[24] Mastin, Luke. *Speed of Light and the Principle of Relativity.* 2009 The Physics of the Universe http://www.physicsoftheuniverse.com/topics_relativity_light.html

[25] Peat, F. David. *Infinite Potential: The Life and Times of David Bohm*, Reading, Massachusetts: Addison Wesley, 1997, pp. 316-317. ISBN 0-201-32820-8.

[26] Aristarchos of Samos (~ 310 BC - 230 AD) had advanced the heliocentric hypothesis and Copernicus was aware of this and some Islamic scholars had held similar views.

[27] Kepler's laws were not immediately accepted. Several major figures such as Galileo and René Descartes completely ignored Kepler's *Astronomia nova*. Many astronomers, including Kepler's teacher, Michael Maestlin, objected to Kepler's introduction of physics into his astronomy.

[28] A similar story can be told about the Earth being round, not flat: again, already suspected by Greek philosophers (who interpreted the phases of the moon as indicating the shadow of a spherical earth), and by Columbus, but not

actually *proved* until Magellan's circumnavigation of the world in 1519-22.

CHAPTER SEVEN

[29] https://www.deepakchopra.com/

[30] Online Etymology Dictionary – cosmos … from Latinized form of Greek *kosmos*
http://www.etymonline.com/index.php?term=cosmos

CHAPTER EIGHT

[31] Vernon, Mark. *Carl Jung, part 6: Synchronicity.*
The Guardian, 4 July 2011
https://www.theguardian.com/commentisfree/2011/jul/04/carl-jung-synchronicity

[32] Minkel, J R. *Quantum Theory Fails Reality Checks.* Scientific American 18 April 2007
https://www.scientificamerican.com/article/quantum-theory-fails-reality/

[33] Sheldrake, Rupert. *Morphic Resonance*
http://www.sheldrake.org/research/morphic-resonance

CHAPTER NINE

[34] Leadership Classics *Ancient Greek Culture and Civilization.* (2010)
http://www.leadershipclassics.org/AncientGreekCulture&Civilization.html

[35] M. G. J. Beets (1993). "The Road to Larissa a Companion to Plato's Menon."

[36] CAP: *Quest: The Essence of Humanity* (Wiley, Chichester, 2013)

[37] Sir Francis Bacon, "ipsa scientia potestas est" (knowledge itself is power). Meditationes Sacrae (1597).

[38] Allport, Gordon W. Concepts of Trait and Personality. Originally published in 1927, this classic article by Gordon W. Allport highlights the ambiguity surrounding attempts to characterize personality traits.

[39] D'Souza, Steven and Renner, Diana (2014). *Not Knowing: The Art of Turning Uncertainty into Possibility* LID Publishing ASIN B00ZY818Z2

CHAPTER TEN

[40] Live Science, *What Is El Niño* 20 August 2015 http://www.livescience.com/3650-el-nino.html

[41] Hagelin, John S. *Is Consciousness the Unified Field? A Field Theorist's Perspective.* https://www.mum.edu/wp-content/uploads/2014/07/hagelin.pdf

[42] Planck, M. *Where is Science Going?* [with a preface by Albert Einstein], trans J Murphy, Allen & Unwin, London, 1933, p 217; from Iain McGilchrist: *The Master and his Emissary. The divided brain and the making of the western world* (Yale U Press, New Haven, 2009) p 460.

AN INTRODUCTION TO ANDREW WALLAS

ANDREW WALLAS is a successful businessman and intuitive corporate shaman. A pioneer in business leadership, he combines his City experience with deep insight to achieve radical transformation in organizational structure. Through his company, Business Alchemy Limited, he supports businesses to realize their latent potential.

ABOUT THE BOOK

Business Alchemy takes a radical new approach to transforming business. It is not formulaic and does not follow a predetermined path. It is concerned with identifying the hidden aspects of a business that block performance, as well as illustrating how to access infinite possibility and potential. Throughout this invaluable book, Andrew Wallas puts forward a refreshing and exciting approach to business that gives everyone the opportunity to create alchemy.

Following great success with the application of Business Alchemy, Andrew Wallas founded The School for Business Alchemy which provides a one year training in the principles outlined in this book. The training, commencing in September each year, consists of 10 full days throughout the 12 months period and is aimed at senior executives and leadership coaches.